Black Tie Optional
17 Stories

Also by Carrie Jane Knowles

The Last Childhood: A Family Story of Alzheimer's
Lillian's Garden
Ashoan's Rug
A Garden Wall in Provence

Black Tie Optional

17 Stories

Carrie Jane Knowles

Owl Canyon Press

First Edition, 2019

All Rights Reserved

Library of Congress Cataloging-in-Publication Data

Knowles, Carrie Jane

Black Tie Optional: 17 Stories—1st ed.

p. cm.

ISBN: 978-0-9985073-6-1

2018965324

Owl Canyon Press

Boulder, Colorado

ACKNOWLEDGEMENTS
(Alphabetical Order)

Apricots in a Turkish Garden, *Glimmer Train* Honorable Mention Short Fiction Competition, 2014

Are You With Me? *The News & Observer, 1998*

Black Tie Optional, Doris Betts Fiction Competition finalist, 2007

Pinhole Vision, *Glimmer Train* Top 25 Finalist Fiction Open, 2007; *Raleigh Review*, 2015

Sad Shoes, *Glimmer Train* Honorable Mention Fiction Open, 2018

Searching for Clint Eastwood, *Glimmer Train* Top 25 Finalist Family Matters, 2009; *Glimmer Train* Top 25 Finalist, Fiction Open, 2011

Selling Fish, *Glimmer Train,* First Place Very Short Fiction Competition, 1998

SIX, *Glimmer Train,* Honorable Mention, Fiction Open 2015

The Black Siamese Twins Meet Queen Victoria, *The Sun,* 1990

The Hound, *The News & Observer, 2001*

The Jungfrau, *Cardinal: An Anthology of North Carolina Writers,* 1986

The Witness, *Village Advocate* Second Place Fiction Competition, 1984

That's what women do:
We carry both the joy and the burden.
We help. We hold on.

TABLE OF CONTENTS

Sad Shoes

It was 7:15 pm when Vicky pulled out of Huntington, West Virginia and headed towards Charleston. She was dog-tired from paperwork, packing, dragging boxes to her car, and dealing with the director at the funeral home, but she was determined to make it home before daylight, so she pressed on. She wanted more than anything to get home before the sun rose, before anyone would see she had pulled out the seats in the back of her old Windstar minivan and was transporting a shiny pale pink casket across state lines.

Pink had been the obvious choice. The funeral director went along with Vicky's request, even though he indicated more than once that dark mahogany might have been more appropriate for someone of her mother's age, or even one of the more understated and less expensive caskets made of unvarnished pine.

"But," he said more than once. "If cost is not an issue..."

"Mama liked pink," Vicky repeated each time he tried to steer her towards something more subtle. "She had a pink bathroom, a stack of fat pink towels and even a fluffy pink toilet seat. She had pink everything. Took all that pink with her when she went to the retirement home, even her collection of pink candy dishes. Her best Sunday dress was pink. It had ruffles all down the front and a frilly hemline she thought made her look a bit sassy. I kind of wish she was being buried in that dress."

The staff at the retirement home had sent a rather tattered flowered housedress, along with her mother's body, to the mortuary. When Vicky saw how the funeral home had dressed her mother, she was aghast and called up the Sunshine Chateau Retirement Village to give them a piece of her mind on her mother's behalf.

"My mama wouldn't have been caught dead in something as tacky as that flowered housedress!" Vicky screamed at the retirement home director.

"Your mama got right bossy in the end and wouldn't take that green flowered dress off to take a bath, go to bed or get up to eat breakfast. We figured it was her favorite dress, so when we found her dead in her bed, in that dress you're screaming about, we quick pulled it off of her before she got too stiff and sent it to the laundry. We even had them iron it so she would look good for eternity. With all the fuss she made about not wanting to take it off, we figured she'd be happy to wear it for a while longer. Sorry you don't agree."

"She liked pink," Vicky said, standing her ground.

"She liked to have driven us crazy. But, she was a nice lady, although a bit feisty. She didn't care much for vegetables."

"She was ninety-seven," Vicky shot back. "When you're ninety-seven, you can wear whatever you want, say what you want and eat whatever you want. I hope you live long enough to experience all that, and if you do, I hope the person who discovers you dead some morning takes the time and consideration to dig through your closet to find something better to wear than some ugly green flowered housecoat."

When Vicky finished what she had to say about their choice of clothing for her mother, she hung up the phone without bothering to say thank you or anything nice like that. She had already packed what little her mother had left of this world in the back of her car and was ready to get on her way. She had no intention of ever going back to the Sunshine Chateau.

Vicky owed the retirement home money. Four thousand seven hundred dollars to be exact, so she thought it best that she got a little bossy herself in order that no one would dare ask her a second time for the money. She didn't have it on her, didn't have it anywhere, in fact.

Her mother had always taught her that whenever you are in a tight spot, you should be dressed as high in the nines as possible, so no one gets any kind of idea that you can be messed with. And, given the whole pink casket, ugly green housecoat, not to mention, her dead mother situation, she was not feeling like being bossed around.

She believed she had done a good job dressing for the situation at hand. She was wearing a tight black skirt with her best pair of black stiletto heels. She thought her mother would be proud of her. The stilettos were a bit worn at the heels and scuffed, but they were the only black shoes she owned. Plus she thought the ensemble looked respectable. She had never picked up a body at a funeral home with the intention of carrying it over several state lines before, and she wanted to be sure to do things right in order to pay her mother some respect.

Unfortunately, her mother's passing came as a surprise, so Vicky wasn't totally prepared for the whole situation. The only clean shirt she had was red satin, a bit low cut and missing the top button.

"Are you sure it's legal for me to carry my mother home in my van?" Vicky once again asked the funeral director.

"We could do the transport for you in one of our hearses for $1,200; you could buy a plane ticket for her; or put her in your car and take her with you. Whatever you like. But, yes, it is legal."

Vicky did not have the $1,200. And she had never herself had the privilege of flying on an airplane, so she didn't think it was right that she would run up yet another bill on her already burdened credit card just so her mother might fly home in comfort rather than ride with her in the van, even though the heat in the car was a bit hit and miss. When she checked the weather report, it looked like the temperatures in the mountains of West Virginia were dropping and could be well below freezing by the time she hit them. She was hoping there wouldn't be snow. Her tires weren't all that good either.

"She doesn't need to be climate controlled or anything?" Vicky asked.

The funeral director stared at her.

"I mean she isn't going to start smelling, is she?"

"She has been embalmed, if that's what you're asking, and as long as you don't run the heater in your car at full blast the whole way home, you ought to be fine. A little heat won't hurt her, neither will the cold."

Vicky had asked the funeral director if he would pull the pink satin coverlet in the casket up around her mother's shoulders before he closed the lid and locked things up, just in case.

The funeral director rolled his eyes and handed her an envelope.

"What's this?" Vicky asked.

"The bill," he replied. "We normally send it after the funeral is over, but because you are taking her home to rest, rather than having us take care of the final arrangements, I thought I'd give it to you now."

He held out his hand.

Vicky shoved the envelope deep into her purse.

"I'll send it to you as soon as I get home," she smiled.

"I believe we should settle our arrangements now, before you take her," he said.

Vicky wondered what would happen if she just got up, drove off, and left her mother behind.

SAD SHOES

"Credit card?" Vicky asked.

"Visa, Master Charge, Discover, whatever. We are good with any of them."

Vicky dug the envelope out of her purse and opened the bill: a straight up no fuss five grand that she didn't have. She blanched.

"A simpler casket would have cost you less," the director said.

"Mama didn't like wood so much. She liked pink," Vicky said in her mother's defense.

"How would you like to pay?"

Vicky began rummaging through her purse. After some effort, she pulled out three credit cards.

"You can put $1,500 on each of these, which makes $4,500, and I'll send you the other five hundred when I get home."

She said it with as much conviction and style as she could muster. She was hedging her bets that she had that much room on each of the cards. She knew she didn't have $5,000 on any one of them.

"I've got a few things to settle with Mama's estate, and then I'll be good for the rest, I promise."

She crossed her heart and gave him her best smile.

He took the credit cards, ran each through his machine, then handed them back, knowing full well he'd never see the other $500, but $4,500 was more than he thought he'd get from the likes of her, and truth be told, the pink casket had been an eyesore ever since it came into the building. He really should have given it to her at half price.

"I'm assuming you're ready to take her with you?"

"Got a full tank of gas," Vicky said, gathering her coat and purse. She couldn't believe she'd just maxed out every credit card she owned and had no more give to get in her small world of finance. Things had been tight ever since Albert had left her high and dry for some teenager who didn't know any better than to take him in. He sure could talk a good game when he'd had a drink or two. Whiskey always made his eyes look soft and sexy and his voice thick with the suggestion that there was something cooking behind all his promises of love and a good life.

There had been no good life with him and not much love. Instead, their life together had been a steady stream of hung over mornings, lost jobs, and bills. Bills that Vicky paid by working a second job stocking shelves at Wal-Mart three nights a week from midnight to 6am. The tips she made wearing her black high heels and waiting tables at Hooters during lunch were not enough anymore to cover what she owed.

"Shall I pull around to the back?" Vicky asked, jangling her car keys in the hopes of hurrying things up a bit.

"To the side," he said. "There's a ramp there where we can roll her down on a cart and slip her into your car."

Once the casket was loaded in her van, Vicky backed out of the funeral home lot and wove her way through town to the I-64 East entrance heading to Charleston, careful not to let the pink casket slide from side to side too much and throw her van off balance. It was comfortably past the rush hour when she eased onto the highway. The long night stretching out before her was cold but clear.

Once she got on the highway, she felt like she had left her debts to the funeral and retirement homes behind her, and she was beginning to feel like she was on her way to making a fresh start: no husband to deal with and no mother to take care of. Truth was, trying to pay off the bills her ex-husband had racked up and the constant monthly reminder that she owed the retirement home another couple thousand for her mother's care had been hard for her. Maybe now she could quit the

SAD SHOES

Walmart job, hell, maybe find a better joint than Hooters to work in, where the tables might turn a little faster and the tips be bigger. She'd been thinking lately that if she could only get out of debt, she would go back to school, get her GED and study something about computers.

Vicky was hugging the right lane traveling five under the speed limit. Traffic all around her was buzzing by, but she couldn't do anything about it because there was a big slow truck in front of her. She took a deep breath and flashed her lights, hoping he'd get the message to get on with it or get off at the next exit. Nothing. In fact, if anything, Vicky thought he slowed it down even more just to get on her nerves. The driver stuck his arm out his window and motioned for her to pass. She ignored him.

She had no intention of passing him. She was afraid that if she did, the driver might get a good look at her car and see her mother's pink casket in the back. No matter what the funeral director said, she wasn't convinced it was legal for her to carry a dead body across state lines.

About ten miles out of Huntington, a trucker honked as he passed her van and flashed his lights. She flashed back just for the hell of it. He was traveling fast when he passed her and she was pretty sure he hadn't seen the pink casket.

She had purchased a guzzler of Coca-Cola, along with a bag of salsa flavored Doritos and a package of Little Debbie donuts when she gassed up the van before getting her mother. She figured the caffeine in the soft drink would keep her awake and the Doritos and donuts would smooth the edge off her hunger. She hadn't had either enough time or money to eat a decent meal since she got the phone call at Hooters that her mother had passed.

She hadn't planned on stopping for food on her way home. She didn't like the notion of cruising through a fast food joint, putting her mother on display for the gawking curiosity of the cashier in the drive-through, and she didn't want to stop at a restaurant anywhere and leave her mother alone in the car.

Besides, she had no money except from the tips from the day before that she'd thrown into the bottom of her purse, hoping they would be enough to pay for gas and tolls to get her to Huntington and back to Raleigh.

She picked up her opened purse on the seat beside her and gave it a shake to see what she had left.

"Sorry about the pink casket."

Vicky snapped her head to the right and dropped her purse. Coins and bills spilled out onto the floor. The glow from the nuclear power plants dotting the horizon as she drove past the town of Nitro temporarily blinded her from seeing her mother perched on the seat next to her.

"You're kidding me," Vicky managed to say.

"I have to admit I was touched by your generous and thoughtful gesture. It's perfect. Very me. Kind of makes me think you can take it all with you. By the by, that fucker at the funeral parlor was secretly happy you took the pink casket off his hands. He hated it. Even thought about cutting you a half price deal on it. Thought it was an eyesore and detracted from the class of his showroom. He has no flicker of a thought that there's any possibility that you're going to come through with the remaining $500 you owe him. So, that's one debt you can write off. Thought you'd want to know."

"Did the credit cards go through?" Vicky asked.

"Master Card had to extend your credit line another thousand, but they were happy to do so. Seems like you do play your bills, even though you pay them slowly. How's that second job going for you?"

Vicky made it through a soft turn in the road, and when she saw a straight stretch of pavement ahead, she looked in her rearview mirror to see if there was anyone behind her. When she saw the road was clear, she eased up on the gas a bit and turned her attention toward the passenger seat. She was having a little trouble realizing she was talking to her mother. Not her mother, exactly, but the ghost of her mother. She swung her right arm out hoping to catch her mother unaware. Her hand smacked against the back of the passenger seat.

Her mother laughed.

"It's me," she said. "Maybe the best of me even though, excuse the pun, I'm a shadow of my former self!"

Her mother rolled her head back and let out a cackle of laughter.

"How long?" Vicky asked.

"How long am I going to stick around?" her mother asked.

"Yeah, how long am I going to be stuck with you sticking around like this? Can anyone else see you?"

"I'm new at this, but I'm guessing I don't have long. Feels like I'm working on some kind of reserve battery that has a limited shelf life. And as for others seeing me, I'm thinking you're the only one. I was sitting on the casket back there when that eighteen-wheeler passed you about a half hour ago. I waved, but didn't get any response. So, I guess you're it. "

"I'm sorry I wasn't there when you died," Vicky said. "I'd have never let them put that ugly housecoat on you."

"My dancing days and ruffled dresses were over long ago. You ought to get yourself one of these housecoats. Hundred percent cotton. Soft. Comfortable. Easy to put on. Zips right up the front. No buttons. Looks good with slippers. Doesn't squeeze anything. And, it has pockets. Why in the hell don't all women's clothing have pockets? Now, there's something to fight about."

"You're freaking me out," Vicky said, putting both hands on the wheel as though by holding tight she could get control of what was happening.

"About the housecoat?"

"About you. Being here. Talking to me. You're dead and you're supposed to be tucked in tight and locked up in that pink box back there. Let's not forget it cost me extra. Extra that I didn't have, and now I feel like I'm losing my mind."

"Oh, you're fine. Besides, I won't be here long. Just long enough to have my say. And, let me say, that you need to pick up I-77 South. The exit is coming up in a couple of miles."

"You're not supposed to be here telling me what to do," Vicky said as she flipped on her turn signal and gently leaned her van into the curve of the exit that would connect her with I-77. Three more hours driving on the interstate would take her the rest of the way though West Virginia and Virginia and into the northern edge of North Carolina after which she would catch US-52 at Mount Airy to Winston Salem, then get on I-40 to go home. They had an easy six hours of driving to go before she'd be able to pull into her driveway, get a drink and settle her nerves.

"I need to pee," Vicky said.

"Then I suggest you find somewhere to stop."

"And you?" Vicky asked.

"I don't need to pee, if that's what you're asking."

"What do I do with you while I'm in the Ladies Room?"

"How about you leave me in the car. I'd lock it, however, if I were you. People might get curious about the shiny pink casket in back. It's kind of a novelty, you know."

"Lock you in the car? If you could get out of that locked pink casket, you can get out of this beat up minivan. I'm not even sure the locks work. Don't think I've locked this heap in five years. I've been hoping that someone might steal it and give me a shot at the insurance money."

"Don't want to hurt your feelings or anything, but I think you'd be lucky if you got ten bucks for this junker. Lock or don't lock. It's up to you. But, if you need to pee like you said you did, let me suggest you opt for the friendly KFC coming up on your right. I'll follow you in. Even though I'm not hungry and apparently can't eat, I can still smell. I do love the smell of chicken frying. Be nice to have one more whiff before passing on."

"You're sure no one else can see you?"

"Pretty sure."

"The funeral home went a little heavy on the makeup when they did you up. Since when did you start wearing red lipstick?"

"Seems that was all they had. Thought it looked okay. You don't like it?"

"Doesn't quite go with the green housedress thing."

"Hmmm. You can try, but, I don't think you've got a chance of getting it wiped off, unless you've got the key to my crate and can fix…"

"That's okay," Vicky interrupted. "I can live with it if you can."

"Live with it! That's rich…but, while we are on the topic of clothes and make up and all that girly kind of stuff, let's talk about…"

"The red silk blouse was the only clean shirt I had. I'd planned to do laundry today, but…"

"I figured as much. No need to get defensive. My real beef is with the shoes."

"What about my shoes?"

"You think those high heel hooker spikes are appropriate given the sad nature of my situation?"

"Black skirt, black shoes…the only black shoes I happen to own, I might add. What would you have wanted me to wear?"

"Something different. Maybe shoes that didn't look so much like happy party shoes."

"Sad shoes?"

"Yeah, sad shoes, like maybe you're sorry I'm gone. Like maybe you're going to miss me."

SELLING FISH

Miss Ellen at the fish store says she has met God. She was carrying shrimp and croakers from the cooler out back into the store early one Saturday morning and had this terrible pain in her stomach. High in her stomach, she always says when she tells the story. She says it felt like something was tied up in knots inside her and was going to burst. It was early and she was the only one there, so she took her daddy's old pick-up truck and drove herself to the hospital.

When she got to the hospital, the pain was so bad she was afraid she wouldn't make it across the parking lot. Since no one was there to help her, she left the truck right in the circle where the ambulances come to the emergency room, got out and tried to walk through the doors.

"That's when I collapsed," she always says, spreading her hands out flat like she's smoothing the quilt on a bed. "Collapsed right there on that rubber pad that makes the door open when you step on it. Out cold like I was dead."

It's an amazing story. I could hardly believe it the first time I heard her tell it, but I knew it was true because I have known Miss Ellen since she was a little girl and she is not the kind of person to make up things to tell. In fact, she usually doesn't talk very much at all, especially since her daddy passed two years ago. But mostly, until this happened, all she's ever said to anyone when they came into her daddy's store to buy fish was, "Help you? Help you?" It's a rather irritating little call that sounds a bit twitchy when it comes out like she really doesn't mean she's glad you're there, or that she's afraid you might want something she doesn't have. The way she says it makes you wonder if it was what her daddy taught her to say when she was little and learning to sell fish, or just what she thought she ought to say.

Miss Ellen always closes her eyes and takes a deep breath when she gets to the part about collapsing at the door. Miss Ellen is a big woman. She's one of those tall people with little bird legs and a thick-chested body, and although her hands and feet are small and childlike, she walks heavy. You can feel the breath go in and out of her as she takes your fish from the ice and carries it back to where they scrape the scales off and filet it for you.

"I could hear the door opening and closing, opening and closing, opening and closing, like it was the beat of a drum. It kept doing that, opening and closing, opening and closing, because I was lying on that rubber pad. That's all I could hear for awhile and then I couldn't hear the door anymore. In fact, I couldn't hear anything. Then my hands and my face got real cold like it feels when you've been on the beach all day and the sun begins to go down and your face gets all cool when the wind blows against it."

By this time, people are usually pretty quiet because they've never heard Miss Ellen talk so much before, especially about things like how it feels to have the first breeze of the evening blow across your sunburned face.

It is amazing to hear someone you've seen grow up, someone you've bought fish from every week for the past forty years, tell a story like this. It's one thing to read it in a magazine in the dentist office but quite another to hear it as fact.

SELLING FISH

"I have to tell you," Miss Ellen says, opening her eyes and bringing her hands in close to her body the way a bird might tuck its wings. "It was like sleeping in a bed of goose down pillows when the dark of the night is all around you like a hum. And that's what I heard, a hum. It wasn't a song. It was a sound I could feel, you know, like that hum you feel when you put your hand on the refrigerator door."

When she gets to this part, about the sound you feel when you put your palm flat against the refrigerator door, you know she's telling the truth. I never heard about anyone else ever feeling it like this before, so I know this is not something Miss Ellen read somewhere and thought it would be good to throw in just to make her story better. Also, you can see how, when she tells this part, everyone who is listening shakes their hand a little like it has fallen asleep, or like they've felt it too and wondered what it was they were feeling.

"I followed that hum, let my body fall into it a little like you do when a big wave comes and rolls you over in the surf. I didn't feel like fighting it. Didn't want to. Couldn't. Just let myself roll down the tunnel. It was the most wonderful thing I've ever done. It was like I was singing in a great big choir. But I wasn't, and I could hear myself breathing like I was far away, and I had the sense that what was me back there on that rubber pad didn't feel like singing at all."

You need to know that people who live in this part of Raleigh and buy fish from Miss Ellen are not the kind of people who waste time debating about whether or not there is life on Mars, or talk about their feelings to anyone, including their husbands. What happened to Miss Ellen is such a shock that no one ever argues with her story or stops her to ask if maybe she was drinking or dreaming or both. The whole thing is nothing but powerful.

"That's when I saw Daddy. I looked away for a minute from my breathing-self, lying on that rubber pad, to the hum, and there was my daddy. He looked the same, just like he looked everyday of his life when he was alive, even had on his tall rubber boots, the ones he always wore at the store because he said he couldn't stand to have his feet wet and cold from shoveling ice onto the fish all day. Grandma was there too and Daddy's brother Eddie. They were both standing with him on the edge of something; standing in a line like they were there to make sure no one could pass them.

"Daddy was the only one who spoke, the others just stood there. Grandma had her hands out in front of her like she was getting ready to catch one of her grandchildren in her big apron. Uncle Eddie smiled at me and just shook his head.

"'Go back,' Daddy called out to me. 'Don't come any closer. You've got stuff you need to do yet.'"

Like I said, I've known Miss Ellen all her life and she is not the dramatic type. Even when she was little she was proper and lady-like, which is why everyone has always called her Miss Ellen. She's quiet. Big like when she laughs, but quiet most other times, and you know she's missed her daddy.

Miss Ellen never had the kind of mother you'd want to get to know. I went to school with her mother, and I can tell you for certain that she was trash long before she left that little girl. Miss Ellen's mother was always full of excuses for what she did. Said she couldn't stand living and sleeping with someone who always smelled like fish. But that's no excuse to leave your little girl.

It's one thing to leave a man, another to leave a child. Miss Ellen's daddy was too proud to even act mad when his wife left, and too ashamed to ask for help. That's when Miss Ellen started selling fish at the store on Saturdays and after school. I guess she didn't have anywhere else to go. So, it is no surprise that the first person Miss Ellen would see standing in front of the pearly gates of heaven would

SELLING FISH

be her daddy.

"What do I have to do, Daddy, but sell fish?" Miss Ellen says with a laugh that sounds like a question. "What is there to do but sell fish?"

Apparently her daddy never told her what it was she had to do, or if he did, she couldn't hear it because just as quickly as she fell into the dark deep humming place, she got snatched back.

"There was this terrible roaring sound and a pounding in my chest and my head. I heard this little bleep, bleep, bleep and people everywhere talking and running and touching me, and I knew I'd come back. That's all. But, I still don't know what I'm supposed to do but sell fish."

I have lived in Raleigh all my life and except for when I was sick or away visiting, I have gone to the Renewed Hope Baptist Church every Sunday and every Wednesday evening. When I was little, the Renewed Hope Baptist Church only had metal-folding chairs; then later, after we had the big building fund drive, we got wooden pews. The wooden pews are warmer to sit on, but not much softer. Sometimes I think all I've done in my life is sit in church and squirm.

Until Miss Ellen told her story, I had never considered the possibility of meeting God. It is hard for me to figure if I was to go like she did, if I would be welcomed or sent back.

Right after Miss Ellen started telling what happened, lots of people came from all over to buy fish. People started thinking Miss Ellen was going to be famous and would probably be asked to be on Oprah or at least the morning talk show on WPTF radio. But, nothing ever came of it. Miss Ellen didn't even get her picture in the local paper or anything, and mostly just the people who always shopped at her daddy's store go there now.

Miss Ellen still greets everyone the way she always did, calling, "Help you? Help you?" when they step up to the counter to look at the fish. But it doesn't get on your nerves the way it used to. It sounds different since she came back, not at all like words, but more like the song of a small brown-feathered bird just happy to have found a place on a fence to rest.

SEARCHING FOR
CLINT EASTWOOD

"I haven't worn underwear since I moved away from home in 1936. Ask Aunt Doris."

"Are you sure you don't wear underwear?" I asked, continuing to pack her freshly washed bras and panties into her suitcase.

"Why on earth are you talking about underwear?"

"You were talking about underwear."

"I was not."

"Tell me again," I said, "about your cousin, Clint Eastwood."

Clint Eastwood was my mother's favorite topic. As her memory steadily unwound itself backwards, she had become more and more unreliable, but had never let go of the notion that she was related to Clint Eastwood.

For the record, Aunt Doris, my mother's older sister, has spent her life refuting my mother's claim and loudly proclaiming the reason my mother believed Clint Eastwood was her cousin was because Mom was boy crazy. Which explained why my mother had collected three husbands in an otherwise busy life of raising me alone.

My father was her first husband. He ran away right after I was born. I never knew him. The second husband, a very quiet and polite man, was with us for about two years before he surprised us both by running away with Mr. Winters, the junior high school principal. Her third husband died of a heart attack shortly after he moved into our house with his laconic basset hound, Garrett. When I moved away from home, I took Garrett with me.

Throughout her various marriages, my mother worked in the high school cafeteria and never missed a day. I suspect she'd be working there still if she hadn't tried to bake the frozen pizzas without taking them out of the boxes and nearly burnt down the cafeteria. That was six years ago. She was 82 at the time.

She was an easy fifteen years past retirement but kept on showing up every morning to work. The school foolishly let her stay. In any case, the burning pizza boxes made a horrible stench and a lot of smoke before they actually burst into flames. Fortunately, the staff was able to clear the building before anyone got hurt. The fire department had to drag the hoses through the cafeteria to the kitchen to douse the flames and told the principal that either they get rid of Mom or risk being shut down altogether.

Right after the pizza fire I figured out Mom had Alzheimer's and pretty quickly moved her out of her house and into an Alzheimer's facility. Even after she moved, Mom kept insisting she needed to go to work. In order to keep her happy, the staff at the home gave her an apron and a job in the dining hall. Every morning at 7 a.m. on the dot, she'd show up at the kitchen door, her apron tied around her nightgown, ready to go.

Her job was to fill the cracker baskets. She liked counting crackers: twelve to a basket. Twelve, she'd always tell me, pointing to the baskets whenever I'd join her for a meal. You have to put twelve in each basket.

I gave the kitchen staff an envelop with seven one dollar bills in it every Friday. It was Mom's paycheck. Mom, in turn, dutifully left one dollar each night beside her plate after dinner as a tip.

Having a job and being able to tip the staff made her happy. It was a pretty good system and was working nicely until the Clint Eastwood incident.

This is what happened: Mom knocked Floyd Ellington off of the chair he was sitting on in the television room while everyone was watching the 1969 musical, *Paint Your Wagon,* that charming not so wild Gold Rush musical where Clint Eastwood and Lee Marvin share a wife, Jean Seberg.

While the rest of the residents were happily engaged in singing along with Clint during his wistful love song solo, *I Talk to the Trees,* my mother started talking about Clint Eastwood being her cousin and Mr. Ellington called her a liar.

I think she'd still be in the Alzheimer's wing counting crackers if all she had done was knock Mr. Ellington off his chair. But, while he lay on the floor, Floyd Ellington (who believed he was related to Duke Ellington despite the fact that he was white and the Duke was black) kept calling Mom a liar. In an attempt to shut him up, Mom, picked up Mr. Ellington's cane and hit him a good whack on the head, knocking his glasses off and taking a chip out of the left front tooth of his top denture. Mr. Ellington's family decided to press charges in order to recoup the cost of the dental repairs.

The director of the Alzheimer's wing was rather nice about the whole thing. She told the family she thought Mom might have been provoked into hitting him because Mr. Ellington insisted he was related to Duke Ellington. The family agreed to settle on half the cost of the denture repair with the condition I take Mom away for a bit so Mr. Ellington would have time to forget what happened. That's one of the good things about Alzheimer's: they do forget.

Keeping Mom at home was no picnic, so I decided to take Mom

on a trip to meet Clint Eastwood. I asked Aunt Doris to join us, but she refused to come along. I thought the three of us could have had a good time of it, besides, it would have been nice to have Aunt Doris along to keep Mom honest or at least straighten out her stories.

"He was a Cooksey. We were Benders. The Cooksey's were my mother's people, not my daddy's. Everybody said that the Cooksey girls were the prettiest in town and the Bender girls the brightest."

"So his mother was a Cooksey," I pressed, waiting to see if Mom took the bait.

"I said my mother's brother was a Cooksey, and he was a real mean son of a bitch. All the Cooksey people were delicate and fine boned. My mother's brother was tall like Eastwood and so mean we never ever called him by his first name, which was Clarence. We always called him Uncle Cooksey instead."

"And he was Clint Eastwood's father."

"That's what I've been trying to tell you. Uncle Cooksey was his father."

I nodded my head so Mom would keep spinning the story of how her Uncle Cooksey, according to her, had taken advantage of a young girl in town, and the child from that rash moment was Clint Eastwood.

"You can see it in his bones and those beautiful blue eyes," she said, drawing her freshly manicured nails across the picture of Clint Eastwood she'd cut out of a People Magazine. I thought it would be good to get her nails done before we went to meet him.

"Look," she said, smoothing Clint's picture on the table in order to show it to me for the hundredth time. "Look at his face. That's a Bender face if I ever saw one. Look at that jaw. And look, his ears, they're just like mine and like yours. All the Benders have attached earlobes. Kids used to call them vampire ears."

"I thought you said he was a Cooksey."

"My mother was a Cooksey before she got married, and then she was a Bender. All the Bender kin look exactly like her and have these odd ears."

"Like a Cooksey."

"Exactly. When are we going to have lunch?"

"We just had lunch."

"I didn't eat."

"You had a chicken sandwich and a coke. Remember?"

The deal with Mr. Ellington's family was that Mom couldn't go back to live in the Alzheimer's unit until she quit talking about her cousin Clint Eastwood. Hard as I tried, I wasn't making much progress on that score, so I decided it might be good to take a trip to find Clint and settle the matter. Besides, I wanted to find out for myself if he really was our cousin.

Just talking about Clint Eastwood seemed to make everyone in the Alzheimer's wing angry, even the staff. Apparently, everyone wants to believe they are related to someone handsome or wonderful, anyone, except for their real families. If you want to know the truth, I think they were a bit jealous Mom had Clint.

"Who was the girl?" I asked, hoping to get a fix on exactly how I was going to prove her kinship to Clint Eastwood if we actually found him. I honestly didn't think it was enough to point out we all had blue eyes and attached earlobes.

"What girl?"

"Clint Eastwood's mother."

"She was his mother."

"What was her name?"

My mother picked at the small wooly balls on the sleeve of her sweater.

"Uncle Cooksey was a bad one, always touching the girls."

This was more information than I really wanted.

"What say we go find him and say hello?"

"Uncle Cooksey?"

"Clint Eastwood."

"Now you're talking."

My plan was to take a couple weeks off of work and drive with Mom across the country from North Carolina to Carmel, California to meet Clint Eastwood. I had always wanted to drive across the country and figured we could stop along the way to see Aunt Doris in Paducah, Kentucky. Although Mom's memory was pretty scrambled and you wouldn't trust her with a book of matches, she still had most of her language and could hold a conversation as long as no one asked any questions or called her a liar. She was fun in her own way even if she could be a bit off the beaten track with her facts.

Mom's memory wasn't getting any better. In fact, it had recently taken a sharp turn to the left and had me thinking I really ought to take her to see her sister before Mom completely forgot she had a sister.

Doris was three years older than Mom and still sparking on all cylinders, despite the fact she had become a bit cranky of late and had refused to come see her sister ever since Mom went to the Alzheimer's unit. Aunt Doris said crazy people were depressing. She was also fond of saying she didn't go anywhere where she couldn't have a shot and a beer on a Friday night, which is why she sure as hell wouldn't ever live in an old folks' home.

I wanted Mom to see Doris before she completely lost her memory. From what I'd read in books, I figured Mom was at that stage in Alzheimer's where she had probably forgotten all the disappointments of her adult life and could enjoy the time when she was young and full of dreams. If nothing else, with any luck, Mom and

SEARCHING FOR CLINT EASTWOOD

Aunt Doris would have a good time telling stories about what they did when they were younger.

Mom and I had not always seen eye-to-eye on everything. I hoped the trip out to Carmel might bring us closer together before it was too late. I wasn't really sure Mom had ever forgiven me for selling her house and putting her in the Alzheimer's unit. And, I wasn't sure she and her sister Doris had talked since the pizza incident. For what it's worth, Aunt Doris and Mom are all the family I have and I wanted more than anything for the three of us to be together again.

"You ready?" I asked, shutting Mom's suitcase.

"For what?"

"To go to Carmel to see your second cousin Clint."

"Go where?"

"To Carmel."

"Caramels stick to my teeth. I don't like them."

I had given Aunt Doris a cell phone for Christmas thinking it might be a good thing for her to have in case she ever got lost or was in an accident or something. She was going on 91 and still driving her 1995 Olds 88 around town. It made me a little crazy. Uncle Ted had died twenty years before, and they had never had any children. I couldn't for the life of me figure out why, if I was the one who was supposed to take care of her, she insisted on staying in Paducah where Uncle Ted once owned the drugstore. In any case, I felt the cell phone was a step in the right direction. I programmed my number into the speed dial before I sent it to her.

Aunt Doris was not shy about mashing on that speed dial button.

"You coming?" she shouted into the receiver.

"No need to shout."

"You sure you can hear me?"

"I hear you fine."

"How's old bar-be-que brains?"

"Your sister is fine. Says she looks forward to seeing you."

"I bet she does. Still talking about Clint Eastwood?"

"We're going to go see him."

"You're as crazy as she is. Where are you going to find him?"

"He's in Carmel."

"And what makes you think he wants to meet the two of you?"

"We're leaving tomorrow morning. Think we'll be at your place on Tuesday."

"I play bridge on Tuesday."

"What time will you get home?"

"Depends if I go to get my nails done or not."

"She's your only sister."

"Thank God."

"We'll be there around supper time."

As luck would have it, a few hundred miles out of Raleigh, Mom saw a sign for a place called the Scottish Inn near Boone and insisted we stop for the night. She started jabbering about how the Benders are Scotch-Irish and we owed it to them to stay at their house. I told her I didn't think we're really Scotch-Irish at all and even if we were, the Scottish Inn had nothing to do with her family. She insisted, so we stopped.

When I found our way to the hotel I notice there was a theatre right across the street from the hotel showing Clint Eastwood's latest movie: *Gran Torino.*

"Let's go see Clint Eastwood tonight," I said, unloading our bags from the car.

"He's here?"

I was a little tired and pretty worn out from listening to the same story over and over again about how she and Clint Eastwood were not only cousins, but kissing cousins as well. Again, more information than I wanted to know told a few too many more times than I wanted to hear it.

"No, at the movies, there," I pointed, at the sign across the street a tad more agitated than I had intended.

"I don't see him," she says, starting to get edgy.

The director of the Alzheimer's wing had warned me to watch for little things that could set off Mom. I was watching, all right, but she had forgotten to tell me what to do if things started going wrong.

I decided the best tactic was to stay calm and talk softly like I might do if I was talking to a scared child or a skittish animal. Since she'd come to live with me, Mom and I had spent a lot of time together watching the show about the dog whisperer on the nature channel, and I felt like I had learned a thing or two that might apply.

I took in a slow easy breath.

"I was thinking we could go grab a bite to eat then catch the early show at the movies. There's a movie theatre right across the street and Clint Eastwood's new movie is playing."

"What's playing?"

"*Gran Torino*. Clint Eastwood is in it, probably directed it too."

"Clint Eastwood is my cousin."

"I know."

There was a Perkins Restaurant right next to the Scottish Inn. I put the bags in the room and told Mom we could walk to the restaurant, then cross the street to the movie.

Dinner was kind of a mess. Mom had recently given up on using eating utensils and now preferred to eat with her fingers, dipping whatever food I'd cut up for her into whatever sauce or condiment was on her plate. In preparation for this eating ritual, I had the waitress bring a bowl of blue cheese dressing and a couple other small bowls where I could squirt some mustard and ketchup. I cut Mom's food in strips so she could pick up the food, dip, and eat to her heart's content. By the time Mom had worked her way through her bits of lettuce, her French fries and the fish sticks from her senior citizens meal, the table looked more like she'd been finger painting than eating. I felt so bad about the mess I left the waitress a ten dollar tip.

As soon as we got our tickets for the movie Mom started talking about being hungry and asking when we were going to eat. I tried telling her we just finished dinner, but she failed to believe me even after I told her about cutting up her food in strips so she could dip the strips in the sauces. I also pointed out the collection of sauce on the front of her shirt as proof of having eaten. Big mistake. Mom got even angrier and more insistent she hadn't eaten. I tried to focus her attention on seeing Clint Eastwood.

Like Mom, I've seen all of Clint Eastwood's movies, even the very early ones like *Revenge of the Creature* and *Lady Godiva of Coventry* in which he played a lab technician and the first Saxon, respectively, and didn't even get credited. I guess you could say I grew up with Clint Eastwood. In some way, seeing all his movies over and over again, especially after Mom bought a VCR and we could watch them any time we wanted, I had come to feel like he really was part of our family.

"I'm hungry. I haven't eaten since yesterday," Mom shouted.

People were beginning to back away from us and look at me suspiciously.

"We ate five minutes ago, remember?"

"No we didn't."

"Would you like some popcorn before we go see Clint?" I asked, stroking her arm lightly, as though we were having fun together.

"I want some popcorn and a drink and a box of those pink and yellow almonds."

After Mom moved in with me it didn't take long for me to throw out all my rational good intentions regarding decent dietary habits and what was "good" for Mom. I quickly learned if Mom wanted to eat, then I should let her eat even if she had just finished dinner two minutes before. Sometimes it was the only way to have a little peace in my life. Besides, I'd already tipped a waitress $10 to clean up from dinner so buying a jumbo bucket of popcorn, a drink and some candied almonds for another $10 or so didn't seem like such a big deal to get her to shut up.

Popcorn, candy, drink and Mom in tow, I made an executive decision to sit in the back row of the theatre in case Mom spilled the popcorn and/or the drink or the almonds or got agitated and antsy. It was a good choice.

There was a movie trailer for *The Wrestler* before *Gran Torino*. Two seconds into the preview, Mom started losing it.

"That's not Clint," she shouted. "You told me you were bringing me here to see Clint Eastwood. Who's that ugly man with the scars on his face and that dirty scraggily hair? Clint would never have his picture taken with dirty hair like that."

"That's Mickey Rourke."

"He should get a haircut."

"It's part of his persona."

People in front of us began turning around. One woman even pressed a finger to her lips and did that hushing, hissing, shushing thing and even threw in a long cold glare on the off chance Mom had missed the point. Mom rattled her box of almonds at the woman. I smiled and put my hand on Mom's arm.

She shook it off.

"You told me Clint would be here."

"He will. Just wait."

Just wait. I loved how wonderfully self-possessed and handsome Clint was as Rowdy Yates in *The Magnificent Stranger*. And, how in control and righteous he was as Marshal Jed Cooper in *Hang 'Em High*. Both Mom and I absolutely adored him as the totally cool bad cop Harry Callahan in *Dirty Harry, The Enforcer, Magnum Force, Sudden Impact* and *The Dead Pool*. And, we both said if Robert Kincaid in *The Bridges of Madison County* had knocked on our door in the middle of the night, we would have let him in, no questions asked. The memory of spending just one night with him would have been enough to hold onto for the rest of our lives.

On the other hand, by the time he played Frank Corvin in *Space Cowboys,* his hair was slate gray, there were some serious wrinkles mapping his face and you noticed the attached earlobes a little more. In his defense, Clint was seventy at the time and both Mom and I calmly discussed how hard it must be to sit on a horse, or chase bad guys on a movie set with all those lights beaming on you for all those years without getting a little sun lamp exposure and a few too many wrinkles here and there.

A couple of years later we had a rather large disagreement about him as Frankie Dunn in *Million Dollar Baby*. Mom thought he was a bit too old for the part. Also, she was adamant that he should have never let that young girl fight. I was pretty swept away by the whole thing and said Frankie Dunn was a hero.

If truth be told, by the time Clint played Frankie Dunn, there were more than a few new wrinkles on his face. His voice had also turned to gravel, but, in all fairness, he was still Clint and his eyes still sparkled and I still would have let him in if he had knocked on my door.

SEARCHING FOR CLINT EASTWOOD

Nothing, however, not Frank Corvin or even Frankie Dunn had prepared me for seeing Clint as Walt Kowalski in *Gran Torino*. The opening scene in the church, with him standing by his wife's coffin, was a shocker: his face stern and his wrinkles cutting deep swaths through his face then folding haphazardly down his neck. Plus, there were those skinny arms and the way his lips had all but disappeared into that hard gash of his mouth. Not to mention the leathery turtle-slits for eyes and the shock of thinning grey hair. He just wasn't the same man.

"Where's Clint?" Mom shouted near hysterical.

"There," I whispered, pointing with my right hand, the one that held her popcorn.

"That's not Clint. That's not my Clint."

The shushing woman turned and hissed again, this time so loud, the whole audience turned around.

Mom jumped to her feet, knocking the popcorn bucket out of my hand. Popcorn went flying everywhere.

"Where's my Clint? What have they done with my Clint?"

"Take her out of here," the hissing woman started screaming.

We left the movie. By then, Mom was agitated to near hysterics.

"What's happened to my baby, my baby Clint?"

"It was a movie Mom."

"I want my baby, my baby."

She kept hugging herself with her arms, talking about her baby and rocking back and forth. She wouldn't go into the hotel room. When I tried to touch her, she swung her arm out like she might hit me if I got close.

"Doris knows who took my baby."

"I'm your baby," I said, trying to calm her, "and I'm here."

"No," she screamed, "no, no, no. I want my beautiful baby boy."

After a bit of a struggle, and with some help from the night desk clerk, I got our bill paid and both Mom and our luggage safely back into the car. It took about an hour or more of driving before Mom got so tired of crying she fell asleep, and when she did, I called Doris.

"What happened," Doris shouted into her cell phone.

"I took Mom to see Clint Eastwood's new movie, *Gran Torino*."

"Thought he looked a little too old to be playing around in the movies still, even if he had decided he'd take some kind of corny Pollock name like Walt Kowalski."

"Mom didn't recognize him."

"Recognize who?"

"Clint Eastwood."

Doris didn't say anything. I could hear her clicking her top denture back and forth a little with her tongue. It was a nervous habit of hers: something she did when she was trying to assess a tricky situation.

"Aunt Doris," I said slowly, hoping to get an answer while trying to decide how much I really wanted to know. "Mom started talking about a baby. A baby boy. She said you knew where it was. She said only you knew."

"I wondered," Aunt Doris said, her voice soft and flat, "exactly how long it would take before she remembered."

I drove through the night. Mom slept a few hours, woke, started crying again, asked about her baby then eventually cried herself back to sleep. I was afraid to stop.

It was early morning, six or so, when I pulled into Aunt Doris's driveway. The porch light was on as well as all the other lights in the house.

When I pulled into the driveway, Doris came running out. Mom woke up.

"Dorey, Dorey, Dorey," Mom started crying. "Who took my baby?"

Aunt Doris opened Mom's door, slipped her arm around Mom's shoulder and gently lifted her from the car.

"You remember, don't you? You couldn't keep him."

"Uncle Cooksey," Mom said. Tears streamed down her raw face.

"Yes, Uncle Cooksey."

"They didn't believe me."

"I believed you. You know I always believed you."

I pulled the luggage out of the car and carried it into the house. Aunt Doris had made some biscuits and gravy and was scrambling eggs.

"You hungry?" she asked, looking first at me, then at Mom.

"I haven't eaten in days," Mom said.

"Thought you'd like some biscuits and gravy, a little scrambled eggs. Made you some hot cocoa too."

"You made me cocoa when I came to St. Louis."

"Yes," Aunt Doris said, looking at me and nodding her head.

I sat at the far end of the table and listened. Mom ate, struggling with her fingers and the scrambled eggs, but Aunt Doris didn't say anything about the mess. She just kept talking in this quiet voice agreeing with whatever Mom said. Every once in awhile she'd wipe the tears from Mom's face with her napkin, then feed her bits of biscuits and gravy.

I didn't say anything. I looked at Aunt Doris from time to time and tried to nod occasionally to let her know I was listening and would wait until later to ask questions.

Mom talked a lot about Uncle Cooksey and about going away to some school. She talked about Clint Eastwood, and she talked about the baby and when she did, she cried. Sometimes Doris listened quietly and other times, she moved her chair closer to Mom and held her shoulders and rocked her.

"You remember when I came to St. Louis?"

"We had fun," Aunt Doris said, smoothing Mom's hair away from her face so she could look at her eyes. "Do you remember that German restaurant? We had liver dumplings and that wonderful red cabbage sauerkraut."

"That was the first time I ever went to a fancy restaurant."

"Me too," Aunt Doris said, tipping Mom's chin up with her fingers and brushing her hair aside.

I could see she was studying Mom's face. I wondered what she was looking for.

"All those forks and spoons. Remember how you got mad at me because I put that piece of bread in my purse."

"I wasn't really mad."

"It was black."

"Pumpernickel."

"I liked that black bread. I'm tired."

"Would you like to go to sleep? I got the guest room all ready for you. Put on Mama's old feather comforter that you always liked."

"Doris?"

"Yes."

"Who was that man you took me to see in St. Louis?"

Aunt Doris kissed my mother's forehead.

"He was a man I knew who I thought would help you forget."

"Yes," my mother said, "that's right. He taught me how to forget."

When Aunt Doris got back from putting Mom to bed, I was cleaning up the kitchen.

"Get yourself a fresh cup of coffee," Aunt Doris said, motioning towards the pot. "Pour me one too. I guess you didn't drive all night long just to eat cold biscuits and gravy."

"Who was the man Mom asked about in St. Louis?"

"Daddy should have never made her give that baby away. She wanted that baby. She didn't care whose it was or what anyone thought."

"It was Uncle Cooksey's?"

"That's what she said, but no one believed her."

"She said you believed her."

"Not at first. Then one day, I was out in the chicken coop gathering eggs and Uncle Cooksey came in, backed me up against the wall with his big ol' disgusting belly and started touching me. I slapped him good right across his fat face and looked him in the eye and asked him if the baby was his."

"What did he say?"

"He tipped back his big stupid head and laughed. I kicked him hard as I could right in the crotch. He never came back for more and he never touched your mother again."

"She had the baby in 1936 didn't she?"

"She was only fifteen when the baby was born. Daddy sent her away to stay with this lady he knew who took care of things like babies who weren't wanted."

"And she wouldn't let her wear underwear."

"We couldn't afford proper maternity clothes for her. Funny the things that get stuck in your brain."

Aunt Doris got up from her chair, poured her cold coffee into the sink and turned on the water to rinse her cup.

"Who was the man in St. Louis?"

"She was never right after that. It was like giving that baby away, even if it had come from no good, broke her. I had left home by then and was living on my own in St. Louis. I had this tiny apartment. It wasn't much bigger than a closet, but I told your mom she could come live with me. I kept telling her that no one in St. Louis would know about her and the baby and she could start all over again."

"And the man?"

"She wouldn't quit crying. I got her a job working in the laundry with me. We ironed shirts. It was hard work standing on your feet eight, ten hours a day, with that hot iron, all those nasty starched shirts. When I married your Uncle Ted, I told him I'd cook and I'd clean, but I was never going to iron another shirt as long as I lived."

"Who was the man?" I asked again, hoping to bring Aunt Doris back on track.

"He called himself Dr. Simon. He had an office above a fancy German bakery in downtown St. Louis. The place smelled like cinnamon and butter frosting. He had a little office with a desk, a chair or two, and this big leather couch. He said he could fix your mom. He said he could hypnotize her, make her forget about the baby and about anything else I thought she needed to forget."

"Like Uncle Cooksey."

"Yeah, like Uncle Cooksey."

"What happened?"

"I don't know. I waited out in the hallway. He had a chair out there where people could wait. I took her to see him a couple of times and eventually she quit carrying on about that baby boy. I asked Dr. Simon once if what he'd done was erase the baby from her brain. He said no, he only moved the memory to a secret corner."

"That's why you wouldn't come, when I asked you to go with us to Carmel, isn't it?"

"I knew she'd find it again. Knew it sure as the world when you said she started talking about not wearing underwear."

"And Clint Eastwood?"

"There were rumors. Kind of like those rumors about Elvis being alive and living in Kalamazoo. Hard to tell if he really is related to us."

"What do you think?"

Aunt Doris dried her hands. She reached into the pocket of her apron and brought out an old newspaper clipping. There was a tall lean young man staring out from the picture. His hair was dark brown, maybe even black, and it was brushed back from his face. Even though the picture was black and white you had the sense his eyes were steely blue and intense. He could have easily passed for a young Clint Eastwood.

I took the picture from her hands. It was the type of photograph you often see in an obituary. It was faded and had a kind of smeary look to it old newspaper photographs get over time, but I could still see my mother's face in his. I could see the odd, slightly elongated earlobes attached along the jaw and the way the skin always felt a little tight over my own cheekbones if I got too much sun.

The name under the picture was Bertrand Anderson and it gave the date of his birth as May 15, 1936 and the date of his death as June 23, 1998. Sixty-two. My brother was sixty-two when he died. There were so many times in my life I had wished for a brother and now I had one that I'd already lost. It made me feel sad and alone in the world.

"I saw him once. I near fainted. The way he walked, just like Uncle Cooksey, and the way he held his head to the side as if he was a bit hard of hearing in one ear, like your mother does."

I handed the picture back to her.

She took it from my hands and carefully unrolled the curled edges with her fingers as if by unrolling them she could make the picture bigger, could make Bertrand come to life.

"Saw him walking down the street in downtown Paducah, big as you please. Thought for a moment he might be looking for me. My name was on those papers, you see. Your mother was only fifteen, not old enough to sign the papers, so Daddy sent me to sign them and to bring her home. The Andersons, the people who wanted to adopt him, were there. They seemed nice enough. Mr. Anderson was kind of short and wore this dark suit with a clean white shirt. I asked him if he was a banker and he said no. He said he owned a haberdashery. I had never heard that word before and had to ask him twice what he said. His wife was tall and thin and sat straight and quiet in her chair. The woman who ran the place brought the baby into the room and gave him to me. She put him in my arms like he was mine. I could hear your mother crying. She was locked in her room down the hallway.

"Bertrand was the most beautiful thing I'd ever seen and he smelled new like freshly ground flour. My name was on the papers as the mother and I had to pretend he was mine. I knew I was supposed to do this thing where I said, 'I give this baby to you.' That's what they told me to say: 'I give this baby to you.'"

"Did she know?"

"When Daddy told her I'd done it, she said she was going to kill herself. That's when I took her to see Dr. Simon."

"And you told him you wanted her to forget you gave her baby away."

Aunt Doris slowly shook her head yes. Tears were streaming down her face. She folded up Bertrand's picture and tucked it back into her pocket. I put my arms around her.

"Do you think she could forget again?" she whispered as though there was something dark and shameful about her wish.

"Yes," I said, "I'm sure of it."

LADY OF THE NIGHT

When the hurricane came in the middle of the night, like a derailed freight train tearing through the streets of Raleigh, Mrs. Lappio got out of bed and put on her dark blue knit dress, her warmest coat, and her sensible brown low-heeled shoes. Once dressed, she pushed her biggest and most comfortable chair into the middle of her living room, opened the curtains on the bay window and waited for the storm to pass.

The electricity had gone out, so she couldn't turn on the television. Instead of sleeping, she sat in the dark and watched the wind blow.

Fortunately, she had not taken off her watch off before she went to bed, so she was able to say for certain what had happened when during the night and give an accurate account of the events of the storm the next morning when her neighbors at last came out of their houses to see the wreckage.

"That big elm there, the one lying across the Morgan's drive, that crushed Mr. Morgan's car, fell at precisely 3:35 a.m.," she told anyone who came by to see the flattened gray Toyota Corolla. "Fell like a dancer, without a sound: the limbs and leaves catching the ground first, easing the trunk down. Then at 3:42 a.m., a small funnel cloud, a twister, came from the middle of the street and tore out that row of roses right there in my yard. Took that big yellow Lady Bank's rose, the one climbing on the fence, pulled the petals and leaves off and flung them into the air like confetti. Then it twisted out the center of that long leaf pine across the street the same way you'd twist off the green top of a carrot. Happened so fast you could smell it before you saw it. The air was filled with the smell of sweet tea roses, pinesap, wet dirt, roots, and red clay.

"Started raining shortly after 4:20 a.m., hard, coming straight down until it hit the wind and got blown sideways."

People would stop for a minute to listen to Mrs. Lappio, shake their heads in disbelief, and keep walking on down the middle of the road. There were power lines torn from the poles laying everywhere. The acrid smell of loose electricity crackled in the morning air.

Mr. and Mrs. Raynes had the front of their porch ripped off by a fallen tree. It was cut clean like someone had sawed it off. It lay in one piece in the middle of their yard.

The Dennings had the massive trunk of a thirty-foot loblolly break through their back roof and cut its way down through their home until it came to rest on their kitchen floor. The root ball of the loblolly was upended and nearly six feet across, standing on end in the backyard. The top of the fallen tree, with its dark green crown of wet pine needles and branches blocked their neighbor's back door and trapped their two cars in their driveway.

Once everyone had a chance to hear Mrs. Lappio's telling of the storm and were able to assess what had happened, it did not take long for people to get to work. The drone of chain saws and the smell of fresh cut wet wood quickly replaced the chitchat and idle wandering of the morning.

Mrs. Lappio had no chain saw or any inclination to work clearing trees and debris. Once the work began, and there was no one to talk to or nothing left to say about what had happened when, she brought out the white wicker rocker from her back bedroom onto her porch to watch as her neighbors cut and cleared. Mrs. Markum brought her a sandwich for lunch. When night came, Mrs. Lappio went back into her home and fell asleep on the couch with her clothes still on. And, she dreamed.

It was a dark dream. A dream of voices and flashes of light and squeals that sounded half-human, half-pig. When she woke at 4 a.m. she had an uneasy feeling that she was in danger.

She checked her windows and doors to make sure they were locked. She opened the curtains in every room so she could see what, if anything, was happening outside. And, she tried again and again, clicking her finger on the button of the telephone receiver, to get a dial tone. She wanted to call her sons, but the phone was dead, and all the lights up and down the street were out. The world was quiet. She knew her neighbors were sleeping the deep hard sleep of people who have survived and could not, or should not, be awakened by her knocking on their doors.

She felt restless.

At 5 a.m., she pulled on her boots, slipped on her old work coat, went out to her shed, got a rake and her gloves, and began to clear her front yard.

There were oak leaves, pine boughs, bits of holly and mistletoe, crepe myrtle branches, magnolia, Japanese maple, poplar, river birch, dogwood, azalea, linden, hedge maple, pin oak, black jack oak, gumball, live oak and willow. It was as though bits and pieces of every species of leafing tree and shrub had made their way into her yard for her botanical classification and pleasure.

There was too much debris in her yard to bag for the garbage men to collect, so she decided to push what she could to the street for the city to pick up.

That's when her rake caught the edge of a raised chunk of broken curb. Mrs. Lappio dug the toe of her boot into the soft wet earth beneath the broken cement and felt something. It was a thick wrist of a root that had broken free of the earth, and in its freedom had cracked the concrete.

She could easily trace the map of the root from the broken curb to the base of the massive pin oak growing ever so close to her sidewalk and her house.

Standing in the street with the rake still in her hand, Mrs. Lappio closed her eyes and tried to remember if she had seen this particular tree swaying in the wind the night before. Had she heard it pop its roots free from the thin layer of cement holding it in place? Had her vigilant watching or her wakefulness kept it from falling?

She had never thought for a minute during the storm that she was in any danger. Even when she saw the big oak in the Morgan's yard come down and crush their car, or when a twister started like a small black swirl of rain and leaves, then spun and tore the rose bushes from her yard. How could she be in danger? She was safe inside her home watching from her window.

But that was then and this was now. She had seen the shallow root clump from the fallen tree in the Denning's yard and knew there was little but dirt in this world holding the big pin oak in the ground. Not knowing what else to do, she paced off the distance from the base of the tree to her home. She then went down the sidewalk in both directions, and out into the street again in an attempt to judge if the tree were to fall, how and where it would fall. There was no question in her mind, once she looked a second time, that if it did fall, it would fall on her.

When she was twenty-seven with two small children at home, Mrs.

LADY OF THE NIGHT

Lappio knew what it was like to have her roots torn from the ground.

Mr. Lappio was thirty then and strikingly handsome: the kind of handsome Mrs. Lappio had loved when she married him. The kind of handsome that made you want to stand close to him, to smell him, to have him whisper to you, and maybe even reach over and touch you when he talked to you.

He was tall, handsome and smart. He looked like someone you wanted to own. The ladies who came into his jewelry store liked the way he smiled at them. The young women who worked in the store liked to stand close to him. Mrs. Lappio didn't like it.

Silly and jealous is what he would always call her when she asked him about the girls he hired, especially the one with the small pearl choker Mrs. Lappio recognized as having come from their store. It was a necklace neither the young woman nor her family could afford.

Silly and jealous, but the girl was tall and thin and had a name like music: Melanie Jamison. Melanie always blushed and looked away when Mrs. Lappio came to the store to see Mr. Lappio.

People in town often saw Mr. Lappio and Melanie together, and they talked, but no one told Mrs. Lappio what they thought. The talk was like bees in an apple orchard, a kind of sweet drone that could put you to sleep if you listened. But Mrs. Lappio didn't listen. She didn't need to. She knew the way her friends looked at her, as if to say they were sorry, that they didn't mean for her to see what they saw...they didn't want to hurt her.

The night after Mrs. Lappio found the broken curb, she dreamt for the first time in a long time about Melanie Jamison. In her dream, the girl was tall like a pine. Tall and thin, and her arms like a ballerinas as she spun and danced. Her green wool plaid skirt twirled around her legs, casting a dark shadow at her feet as she moved down the street in the wind, bending and swaying. Then, in the dream, right before the music came to an end, the girl, Melanie Jamison, began falling. She was falling madly, head over heels, in a wild whooshing somersault that sounded more like a whisper in Mrs. Lappio's ears than the howl of the wind outside.

Just as she always knew she would, Mrs. Lappio eventually found them together sitting over cups of cold coffee in a restaurant. Their heads were bent in whispers, their foreheads nearly touching, and their lips laughing. Mrs. Lappio made a scene. In her memory she clung to the idea that she slapped Mr. Lappio's face and told him never to call her silly again. In truth, she pushed against his shoulder with the heel of her hand and screamed a kind of strangled scream that rang in her ears for weeks afterwards.

Melanie's family sent her to live with an aunt in Greensboro, and Mrs. Lappio took Mr. Lappio back. They never talked about what had happened in the restaurant or could happen again. When their anniversary came around two months later, Mrs. Lappio accepted the gold and sapphire pendant Mr. Lappio gave her, fastened it around her neck and vowed to never take it off. Let it be a reminder to him, she thought, to never call her silly again.

Of course, wearing the necklace didn't work to keep her fears and the other women away. After Melanie left, every piece of jewelry Mr. Lappio brought home for her from the store felt like another woman whispering in her ear.

Mrs. Lappio sat on her front porch and stared at the tree. It had rained every night and into the morning each of the three days after the storm. Her front yard now had the smell and look of a fetid swamp. The storm had brought unseasonably warm weather and the sharp, tart smell of pine pitch. Wet, rotting wood clung to every breath she took.

"Mr. Denning," she called to her neighbor as he walked past her house one morning, "come here, please."

Mr. Denning was not at all like Mr. Lappio. He was small and sturdy and stood with his feet a firm shoulder's width apart on the ground. When he talked, he looked straight at you, and Mrs. Lappio knew, just as she had known Mr. Lappio had cheated on her, that Mr. Denning had never in his married life looked at another woman.

"Mr. Denning!" she called out again. "I need someone to look at my tree," she said pointing to the broken cement at the base of the big oak. "Can you see," she said, putting her hand on the railing and walking down the steps to the public sidewalk, "there, by the street, I think the roots have broken the curb."

"Yes," he said, bending down to look closer. "Must have been the storm. Could have rocked the tree and loosened it a bit."

"Is it safe?"

"Hard to say. I really don't know much about trees. Might be good to ask someone who knows."

Sitting on her porch watching the sun go down across her dark neighborhood, Mrs. Lappio considered what Mr. Denning had said about needing an expert to tell her what to do. She was surprised to realize how little she really knew about anything. She had no idea if the tree that had once been a rather unassuming sapling, but now spread its branches over the breadth and the width of her house, would fall down.

"You can never know," she said aloud to no one, "when something will fall down and destroy everything."

Nothing fell until the end. By then both of their boys were grown and gone and she had a box full of fine jewelry.

That was nearly three years ago. Mr. Lappio was sixty-two at the time and was dying from cancer. From the beginning, the prognosis was not good, but the doctors suggested he try chemotherapy anyway, just in case there was a chance. At the same time, the store was being squeezed out by the competition of the new malls and the chains. Nothing felt right, and whenever Mr. Lappio talked about work, he always complained that no one seemed to care about really good jewelry anymore.

"I'm going to die," he told Mrs. Lappio, one day after the last of his chemotherapy treatments, holding up his hand to her as if to say there would be no discussion about the matter. "So let me have what I want."

"What do you want?" Mrs. Lappio asked as she touched his weathered gray face and his thin gray hands. She wondered what had happened to the smell of him, the thrill of wanting to be close to him and to have him lean over to her and whisper in her ear, knowing no one else could hear him but her.

"I want to be with Melanie."

Mrs. Lappio hesitated before she spoke. Her heart did that odd little flutter it always did when she was tired. She took her hand away from his and let it rest a moment at her throat so her fingers could twist at the gold chain of her necklace and stroke the cool faceted surface of the sapphire.

"If that's what you want," she said.

How long had she known? Maybe always, and in the knowing there had been a sweet but odd tension for her when Mr. Lappio came home every night and lay with her in bed. Did Melanie know he kissed her? Did Melanie know he waited each night to turn the lights off until after Mrs. Lappio had undressed, her clothes falling in a puddle on the floor at the foot of the bed? That he always asked her to take her time pulling her nightgown over her head and shoulders so he could enjoy the drop of the silken fabric down her shoulders, breasts and thighs? Like a spring rain promising flowers, he would say, or a dark sweet dream. Did Melanie know they never once talked about her, ever?

"I will go away each afternoon at two," Mrs. Lappio said in a voice only years of waiting and wondering could control. "Then I will come back at five. She can come everyday when I'm gone, if you like, but the nights are mine, and so is the funeral. I don't believe it is too much to ask...too silly."

"Anything but silly," Mr. Lappio said, reaching out to touch her hand, to draw her close to him for one last time in order to feel the warmth of her face. "I have underestimated you, Mrs. Lappio," he said, letting his lips brush against the soft blond hairs of her cheek. "You are a remarkable woman, a true gem."

For six weeks Melanie Jamison came precisely at two o'clock every day and waited in her car across the street until Mrs. Lappio left the house. And, just as arranged, Mrs. Lappio didn't come back into the house until Melanie's car was gone a little before five.

One day, when Mrs. Lappio came home a few minutes before five, Melanie was sitting in the big wicker chair on the front porch, her hands folded in her lap, her eyes forward, waiting.

"I didn't want you to come in and find him," she said. "He called for you once. I thought you'd want to know."

"Thank you," Mrs. Lappio said. "If you'll excuse me, I have to call the boys."

"Of course," Melanie replied, getting out of the chair. "He wanted me to tell you thank you, and I thank you, too."

It took a week for the city to get the electricity turned back on in her neighborhood, and another day for the phone company to bring back the phone service. By then, both boys had found a way to contact her and make sure she was safe. When she told them about the tree and the broken curb, both of them said she shouldn't take a chance. They told her to make arrangements to have the old pin oak taken down.

That's what she had thought too, except it was planted on that strange little strip of land belonging to the city, in the front of her house between the sidewalk and the curb. So, the tree was a city tree and only the city could decide to take it down. When she called to tell them they should take it down, she was told the city was busy taking care of the immediate storm damage and wouldn't be able to even look at it for months.

That is why, in the end, she called Melanie and asked her to meet her for lunch.

"Were you hit by the storm?" Mrs. Lappio asked.

"Yes," Melanie said. "I lost two trees, one that crashed through the edge of my living room breaking the glass in the windows and causing a leak, the other a small nuisance of a loblolly that fell into the middle of my garden."

"Do you garden?"

"Day lilies mostly, and little bulbs: nothing much, just enough to give me something to weed and look forward to. How about you?"

"Roses. The old fashioned kind that open flat and smell like roses."

"Did your house get damaged by the storm?" Melanie asked politely, which led Mrs. Lappio to tell her about the big pin oak and the broken curb.

"So what do you think?" Mrs. Lappio asked.

"I don't know much about trees," Melanie replied.

"No one seems to know," Mrs. Lappio said, still hoping for the truth.

"It could fall," Melanie offered, "but then you've lived through much worse."

"I have," Mrs. Lappio said, fingering the smooth blue sapphire on its thin gold chain around her neck. "Yes I have, haven't I."

THE HOUND

As she aged and her vision declined, Genevieve's grandmother had worried her lips away to a pale thin line. When her grandmother was younger, she was bold and beautiful and painted her full lips a sweet burnished red to match the polish on her fingernails. Genevieve had loved her grandmother's red lips and shiny nails and had thought she was the most beautiful woman in the world, even more beautiful than her own mother.

But, today was not a day for getting dressed up, wearing lipstick or painting their nails.

"Your mother says I'll get all my meals. They'll bring breakfast to my room and I'll shuffle down to the coffee shop for lunch with all the other old ladies, then over to the dining room for dinner. So take the china."

"I can't take the china."

"Take the china."

Genevieve popped open another packing box and taped the bottom. She unlocked the glass-fronted cupboard and carried the Wedgwood to the dining room table. She then wrapped each dish in packing material and began filling boxes. Neither one of them said anything.

They both knew Genevieve had not come to take the china.

THE HOUND

The Wedgwood plates were flat, perfectly flat and wonderfully smooth to the touch. They were much too fancy for a graduate student, but Genevieve knew that didn't matter to her grandmother. Her grandmother believed you should use the most beautiful things you own every day, no matter what your circumstances.

Among the many fancy things Genevieve loved about her grandmother was that she always put on lipstick when she left her house, even if it was just to go to the grocery store to buy eggs.

Genevieve was her only granddaughter, and they had used the Wedgwood no matter what the occasion or what they ate. Their favorite Wedgwood meals, as they called them, were peanut butter and banana sandwiches, grilled cheese pressed tight in the waffle iron so the cheese would leak out into the crusty waffle dents, and scrambled eggs served with a side of cheese doodles instead of buttered toast.

Genevieve's grandmother walked to the living room. The hound followed her. Genevieve watched as her grandmother ran her fingers over the plants, feeling for dried blossoms and soft dying leaves. She touched and pinched, efficiently moving from plant to plant..

"How many do you have left to pack?" her grandmother called from the living room.

Genevieve looked over the array of unwrapped china remaining on the table, and made a tally.

"The soup bowls are all done. There are five bread and butter plates left to wrap, three luncheon plates, twelve saucers and ten cups."

"It's always the tea cups, isn't it?"

"Usually."

"I broke them both, you know. You never broke any. Broke one on our very first anniversary. Cooked a fancy meal for your grandfather. Chicken cordon bleu, wild rice, and frozen peas. It's so easy to love a man who likes frozen peas. I'd made a fresh blueberry pie for dessert and brewed a pot of coffee. Brought it out to the table on that big silver tray I keep in the bottom of the buffet like we were playing house. He helped me carry the dishes into the kitchen when we were done and I washed while he dried. I guess my hands were soapy, or maybe I was nervous because I had never made such a fancy meal before, but anyhow, when I got to the teacups I dropped one into the dishpan and popped the handle off it. It was the craziest thing. I cried and cried like everything in the world was ruined."

Genevieve had heard the story before and also the story about the time she dropped a teacup one New Year's Eve because she'd drunk too much champagne.

"You've still got ten."

"Wrap one more of the luncheon plates," her grandmother said, tossing the dead leaves into the trash. "We can use the last two for lunch. I'm out of eggs and I haven't had anything remotely as fine as a cheese doodle in the house ever since your mother started buying my groceries. She's pretty strict."

"She can be rather narrow minded about cheese doodles. That's for sure," Genevieve said with a smile.

"I think there's some bread in the refrigerator and a piece of cheese or two that should either be eaten or thrown out. I pulled the waffle iron out of the box your mother packed for the Goodwill. I thought you should have it."

Genevieve had wanted the waffle iron. It was old and heavy and made these perfect little punches in the bread when you squashed a sandwich in it. Her mother never let her grill sandwiches in their waffle iron at home. She said it would ruin it. But, somehow it didn't ruin her grandmother's waffle iron.

Genevieve finished what she had to wrap then put the two luncheon plates on the table and picked out two pale yellow linen napkins from the buffet and two of the etched crystal goblets from the hutch. She knew her grandmother would want to use them one more time. Genevieve loved the goblets and had drunk everything from orange juice to root beer from them since she was old enough to sit at the table and wrap her hand around their elegant stems.

When Genevieve opened the refrigerator door to get the cheese, the hound came shuffling into the kitchen.

"Only one very tiny piece of cheese," her grandmother called out from the living room. "Only one, Genevieve. Sunshine is getting old and the vet has put her on a diet."

"Sorry, girl," Genevieve said, stroking the hound's long silky ears.

"Make her sit. She has manners and just needs to be reminded from time to time to use them."

At the sound of the grandmother's voice, Sunshine sat, chin up, her soft basset ears draped against her stout shoulders.

"Let her have the cheese, then tell her she's a good girl. She can have a little cheese every day. It helps keep her coat shiny. She also likes frozen green grapes and the top stubs from the carrots. Keeps her teeth clean."

Genevieve could hear her grandmother's hands move across the table, checking for a cloth napkin. Her eyesight had gotten worse since her mother took the car away four months ago. Genevieve had told her mother that taking the car away was cruel. She knew her grandmother shouldn't drive, but her grandmother liked having the old blue Cutlass convertible in the driveway. She told Genevieve it made her feel young.

The car was one thing, but Sunshine was another matter. Taking away Sunshine, Genevieve knew, was going to be like snatching the last breath from her grandmother's lungs. It wasn't right, no matter what the assisted living rules said.

"Just a little cheese once every day. She'll want more, but she knows she can't have it. You'll just have to remind her."

Genevieve cut a thin sliver of cheese. Sunshine took it from her hand, dropped it on the floor in order to better examine it, as if she were measuring it, trying to figure if this pitiful offering was going to be it for the day. She pushed the tiny cheese bit once with her nose before picking it up and eating it.

"I told her I couldn't take her with me," her grandmother said. "She's like me, she forgets things sometimes and she doesn't walk very fast, but she can get around the block."

Genevieve dropped a second sliver of cheese onto the rug.

"You'll tell her I couldn't take her, won't you?"

"I'll tell her."

"Hounds don't always remember," her grandmother said, rubbing her lips together as if tracing the memory of red lipstick. "But she'll listen. She's a good girl. She always listens."

DUSK OVER CAIRO

Mrs. Richards called Tina to tell her the police had to break into the house in order to rescue her mother.

"Broke in?" Tina screamed into the phone. Mrs. Richards was deaf, but she never wore her hearing aids. She said they made her dizzy when she put them in her ears.

"Through the kitchen window," Mrs. Richards screamed back. "Stepped all over her dahlias. Broke every one of them. They just bloomed on Monday."

After Tina hung up from Mrs. Richards, she called the hospital to check on her mother. She also called her husband, Will, and told him he was on his own with the kids for dinner. Next, she called her brother, Jerry, and told him he better meet her at the hospital ASAP. She also told him she was canceling all her appointments for the rest of the day and strongly suggested he do the same.

By the time she drove from Pittsboro to Rex Hospital in Raleigh, her mother was already in the recovery room and Jerry was in the hallway talking to his assistant at the real estate office on his cell phone.

"Broke her hip," he said to Tina, covering the mouthpiece of his cell phone.

"Could you please hang up the phone and talk to me?" Tina asked.

"I am talking to you," Jerry said, his hand still covering the receiver while his head bobbed up and down as if the woman on the other end of the phone could see he was agreeing with what she was saying.

"You're not talking to me. You're talking at me like you always do. Could you please hang up and give me one minute of your precious time?"

He ignored her request.

"Before she went into surgery, she said she wanted us to sign an agreement that says we give her permission to starve herself to death," he said, finally clicking his phone shut.

"What'd you do? Sign?"

"Here's my assistant's number if you can't get me on my cell," he said, handing her a business card as if she were one of his clients.

"Thanks."

"Don't let Mom drive you crazy. If you need a break, call Marcie. She's home. Phillip has the flu, but she can get away if she needs to."

"You told her to go ahead and starve, didn't you?"

"I did just what you would have done."

"You changed the subject?"

"Exactly."

"Louise," Tina sang her mother's name under her breath as she stroked her hand and tried for the third time to wake her. "Birds in the trees seem to whisper Louise. Louise. Sweet Louise."

They had given up calling her mom, or mother, as she once preferred, shortly after their father died. Jerry was fifteen at the time and she was twelve.

"Broke everyone of my dahlias," was the first thing Louise said when she at last opened her eyes, her words sticking to her lips a little from the anesthesia.

"Mrs. Richards told me," Tina responded. "She said the police had to break the kitchen window in order to get in."

"Every single one of my dahlias. Just bloomed on Monday. Every single one of them."

"What happened?" Tina asked, reaching for the Styrofoam cup of ice water, holding the straw to her mother's lips so she could drink.

"Got up to pee. Fell and broke my hip. Or, maybe, like the doctor says, got up, broke my hip, then fell. But either way, I had to pee."

"Did you?"

"In a puddle. Throw out the rug. I couldn't get to the phone or the door or even reach the remote for the television. So there I was, in a puddle of my own pee watching CNN. It was like being in some kind of weird broadcast hell."

"How long were you there?"

"All night. Volume on the television was up high too. The remote was in my chair and I couldn't reach it in order to turn it down or off. I had just turned it up when I got up to pee so I could hear it while I was in the bathroom. Had it up loud enough for that crazy Mrs. Richards to hear next door if she'd have been wearing her hearing aids. I lay there all night by myself just wondering if anyone was going to find me or if I was going to die right there with the television blaring."

"I'm sorry," was all Tina could think of to say.

"Old busybody Richards finally comes out to get her morning paper. I guess she noticed I wasn't sitting at the kitchen table having a cup of coffee and doing the Jumble puzzle like I always do, so she got suspicious something might be wrong. Went sneaking around the house looking in the windows like she was expecting to catch a burglar or a murderer."

"She did the right thing," Tina offered.

"I should have moved twenty years ago just to be rid of her. Moved to Alabama or Alaska or someplace where people have enough sense to wear hearing aids if they're deaf."

"She saved your life."

"Saved my life? Crazy woman sees me lying in a puddle on the floor, thinks I'm dead, can't hear me screaming at her to get the key from under the mat to let herself in because she won't wear her hearing aids. So she calls the police and they come busting through my kitchen window and step on my dahlias."

"I'll take care of the rug and call a repairman for the window."

"What about the dahlias?"

"I'll buy you new dahlias."

"They were in bloom."

"I'll find ones in bloom."

Louise had not always been Louise. When their father was still alive, she dressed like a mother, talked like a mother, and even made lunches like a mother. Then she stopped being a mother and started being Louise, and there was very little Tina or her brother could do about it.

Louise began to make some noise and stir a little. She had already awakened twice since Tina had been there, crying, wanting something, anything, to make her feel better. The nurse came in around 11 a.m. and gave her a shot, and told her they couldn't give her another shot for pain again until 4 p.m..

"Hurts," Louise cried out like a child, bobbling back and forth from waking to sleep.

"Birds in the trees," sang Tina, stroking her mother's hand, "seem to whisper Louise."

Louise rolled her head to the music a little and let her eyes come open as her breathing steadied with the song.

"I'm going to die," Louise announced.

"No," Tina said.

"Maybe I want to die."

"Okay, you're going to die."

Arguing with Louise was pointless.

"Don't get smart with me. I'm still your mother!"

Right after their father died, Louise refused to get out of bed for almost two months. Jerry did the laundry during this time because he wasn't afraid to go down into the basement alone. Tina did the cooking, but they washed dishes together because it gave them something to do to pass the time before they got tired enough to go to bed.

Neither one of them knew much about cleaning, so they made a pact not to make their beds or wash the toothpaste off the bathroom mirror, and managed to keep the rest of the house presentable by never going into it.

They left both breakfast and dinner for their mother on a tray on her bedside stand everyday during those two dark months, hoping she'd eat. On the good days the food was gone, on the bad days it wasn't. Tina tried never to think about the many days she carried the food back to the kitchen and threw it away.

"Did you know what was going on?" Tina's husband, who like her, was also a psychiatrist, once asked her.

"That's why," she smiled, "I became a shrink."

"Easier to be one, they always say," he responded, "than it is to go see one."

"Always."

Tina had not needed to go to medical school to know her mother was depressed. She figured that out when she was twelve. So had Jerry. They just never talked about it.

"Why didn't you ever ask?" Louise said when Tina came into her room carrying a fresh tub of ice cubes from the nurse's station.

"Ask what?"

"About then."

"When?"

"When your father died and I didn't get out of bed for two months while you and Jerry fended for yourselves pretending everything was normal."

"What should I have asked?"

"You're good."

"Good at what?"

"At what you do. I knew you'd be."

"Be what?"

"A good shrink."

"So what should I have asked?"

"Why I was depressed."

"I was too young to understand."

"And, now?"

"Maybe too old."

"Your brother wouldn't understand."

"I know."

"I need to tell you something, before I die."

"You're not going to die."

"I had planned to leave him."

Tina had not been prepared for Louise's confession. Despite all her training, and all her many years of psychiatric practice, she could not keep that little flash of shock from showing on her face.

"Surprised?" Louise asked.

"Surprised," Tina conceded.

"He wanted me to be perfect."

"And you weren't?" Tina tried to play it for laughs.

"None of us are."

"Right."

"I wanted passion and he needed me to be perfect to cover for his drinking."

"We knew he drank."

"I know you knew."

"If you knew we knew, then why didn't you talk to us about it?"

"Pretending was part of being perfect."

"I know."

"Two days before I planned to leave your father, he had a stroke and died."

"Had you planned to take us with you?" It was the one question she had wondered about every day of her life since her father died and Louise quit being their mother.

Louise reached across the bed and touched Tina's hand.

"I had a plan for the three of us to escape."

The terrifying fear of being left that had been bottled up inside of her all her life broke like a small glass bubble in her mouth. The taste was salty and painful. Tina squeezed her mother's hand, then leaned over and kissed her.

"While I was lying on the floor by myself, the television blaring, CNN kept playing this old news clip from when Marilyn Monroe died," her mother said. "It was crazy. It was the anniversary of Marilyn's death and they kept playing this one piece over and over again where this reporter describes that her nails were ragged and unpolished when they found her, like that was the one thing we should remember about her. The longer I lay there, the more I started wondering if he wasn't right and if it wasn't the little things, the details like polished nails that get remembered."

"Should I see if they have some nail polish in the gift shop?" Tina asked.

"I'd like that."

While Louise picked at the food on her lunch tray, Tina went to the hospital gift shop to look for nail polish. She took her time looking for exactly the right color.

The last time she had painted her mother's nails was the day Louise finally got out of bed following those two long months after their father died. It was a Sunday, and when Tina brought the breakfast tray into her room, Louise sat up and said she wanted to take a bath and get dressed.

The whole day was kind of like a wonderful dream. Tina and Jerry got out the best towels from the linen closet and ran a hot tub for their mother, filling it with bath salts and bubbles. When Louise finished bathing, she put on her robe and said she wanted to get dressed up fancy and go out for dinner, just the three of them. But first, she told Tina, she wanted the two of them to paint their nails.

Tina, Jerry and Louise drank tea out of their best china teacups and ate toast with peanut butter and grape jelly. When they finished eating, Jerry washed the dishes while Tina and their mother polished each other's nails.

Then Jerry and Tina pulled out all the prettiest dresses from Louise's closet and brought them to the kitchen, one at a time, for her inspection. After much deliberation as to what to wear, Louise finally settled on the rust colored gabardine dress with the crocheted collar. It looked proper, she said, and it matched the color on her nails: Dusk Over Cairo.

Tina and Jerry got dressed in the best they had and the three of them went to the Velvet Cloak Inn to have dinner in the Charter Room. There were tiny yellow roses in a crystal vase at their table. Louise drank a martini, Tina and Jerry had cokes with their meal and chocolate chess pie for dessert.

They laughed and pretended to be rich drinking water out of crystal goblets and eating their pie with tiny silver dessert forks. They talked a lot about the food and how fancy everything was, but nothing else. Ever.

"What color did you find?" Louise asked when Tina came back to her hospital room, a bottle of nail polish in her hand.

"Dusk Over Cairo," Tina smiled wagging the small rust colored bottle in her fingers like the pendulum of a clock.

"That was a wonderful day and a wonderful meal, wasn't it?"

"Yes, it was."

"You promise you'll remember it after I'm gone?" Louise asked.

"Always."

ARE YOU WITH ME?

"Your car has a hundred and eighty-five thousand miles on it, the air conditioning is shot, it burns a quart of oil to every tank of gas, the clutch is beginning to slip, and the last time I drove it, which was yesterday, the brakes felt like mush." Muriel's husband, Alan, wiped the dipstick with a rag and slammed the hood.

"It's never had an accident," Muriel said, defending both her car and her integrity. It had once been Iris' car but now it was hers, and she did not want to part with it, at least not now, and perhaps never.

"Buy yourself a new car," he responded.

"I don't like new things."

"New cars are safe."

"New things are always begging to be broken."

"Says who?"

"Iris."

Muriel did not like change. She did not like that her sister Iris was dying. She felt betrayed by the world.

Iris's hair was falling out from the chemotherapy and it bothered Muriel.

"Don't worry about it," Iris had told her.

"Does it hurt?" she asked.

ARE YOU WITH ME?

"It's hair," Iris said, twisting a thin mound of brown curls in the palm of her hand. "I should have never in my life worried for a minute what anyone thought about what I did or what I wanted to do. Should have dyed my hair bright red long ago just for the hell of it."

"You would have been pretty with red hair," Muriel told her, even though she wasn't sure. She had always envied Iris's beautiful light brown curls.

"I think you'd look beautiful as a blond," Iris said. "Blond and short, kind of casual and sexy in a come-on-world sort of way. Like you'd just driven to the beach in a convertible."

"Really?" Muriel said in surprise. She couldn't imagine doing anything so bold. "What do you think Alan would say?"

"About what?"

"Me in short blond hair?"

"It's hair, Muriel. It's your hair, and you can do what you want with it. Besides, your hair will grow back. Don't you want to live a little?"

"Did you find a car?" Alan asked when she got home.

"No, I went to visit Iris," Muriel replied.

"Thought we talked about you buying a new car."

"Iris is losing her hair. Said she should have dyed it red."

"A red car would be nice."

The next morning Muriel drove to Iris' house, picked her up and took her to the Rite Aid in Cameron Village. Iris had called her that morning to say she needed to buy some baby oil. She said her scalp was hurting from all her hair falling out. Muriel knew that wanting the baby oil was just an excuse for them to look at hair dye.

"What color red?" Muriel asked as they strolled down hair care aisle.

"Too late for me," Iris said, checking the names on the boxes, looking for just the right name and shade. "Thought we could find something for you, some color that will change your life!"

"What are you thinking?" Muriel asked.

"I'm thinking it has to have a good name. Something dreamy. You were always a dreamer."

"Sometimes I dream that the doctors are wrong."

"But, they're not," Iris said, squeezing her sister's hand.

Iris picked Clairol's Moon Haze from the multitude of blond color choices.

When they got back to Iris's house, Muriel was instructed to brush the few remaining strands of Iris's hair from her head, rub baby oil onto Iris's smooth white scalp and wrap it gently in a soft turban. When Muriel finished, Iris told her to sit on the kitchen stool so she could cut her hair and dye it.

"Will it be permanent?" Muriel asked while Iris gently worked the color into her hair.

"Unfortunately," Iris told her, "hair is a lot like life: nothing's permanent."

"What about a sports car?" Alan asked her when he saw her new short blond hair.

"I'm not the sports car type," Muriel responded.

"Sexy blond hair says sports car loud and clear," he teased.

"Enough."

"How about a truck? You used to say you always wanted to own a truck."

"My buying or not buying a car has nothing to do with the kind of

ARE YOU WITH ME?

car."

"There must be something you want."

A couple of weeks later, when Iris became too weak to go out with her for lunch, Muriel asked her what she wanted.

Iris was quick to answer. She wanted a party.

Muriel went to the store and bought blue corn chips and fresh mango salsa, the expensive earth-toned M&M-like candies from the Wellspring, lots of brie and saga bleu cheese, Japanese rice crackers, Iris's favorite chocolate birthday cake from Rebecca's, and bottles and bottles of fairly decent champagne.

Iris wanted the party to be a girl-thing and instructed Muriel to tell everyone they should dress up in their best, polish their nails, make promises, and say their goodbyes. That's what she wanted.

As directed, Muriel put fresh sheets on the bed and decorated Iris's bedroom with buckets of extravagant sunflowers, stargazer lilies, birds of paradise, and heather. Iris wanted lots and lots of heather because she said it smelled like a spring meadow after a cool rain. Iris loved how rain woke the earth and brought it back to life.

While Muriel arranged the flowers, Iris emptied her house of a lifetime of candle collecting. She unearthed tall red Christmas tapers, jasmine scented columns, tea lights, candles pressed with dried flowers she had bought at an art fair, and short squat white ones Muriel had given her, called bogies, to use in case there was a storm and she lost her power.

"It will be a blaze of glory!" Iris exclaimed as she lined her shelves and dresser top with candles. "Tell everyone who we've invited that there are to be no gifts but each of them is to bring me a secret. It will be my gift to them to take their secrets with me so they will never have to think about them again."

"I hated you when I was little," Muriel whispered when it was her turn to step into her sister's bedroom and tell her secret. "Hated that I always had to wear your hand-me-down clothes. That I didn't have my own things."

"I know," said Iris. "Life is short, Muriel. Get rid of my old car. Live your life. Not mine. You deserve better."

"What exactly are you looking for?" The salesman clicked the end of his ballpoint pen as he talked.

"I'm not sure."

"Used or new?"

Muriel drew in a deep breath. "Young, but used," she said. "I'm not quite ready for new."

"Compact, mid-sized, loaded?"

"I'd just like to look."

"Sure, look," he said, his pen clicking and flipping in his hand. "You see something you want to try, the name's Mike."

The last time she and Iris had lunch together they drove around for half an hour trying to find a restaurant that didn't make Iris want to puke.

"Nothing greasy," she said, as they drove past the sweet smoke of a burger joint on Hillsborough. "Let's go for good but not so good that the place smells like curry or garlic. Maybe we can eat outdoors where I can smell some flowers."

Muriel settled Iris into a chair at an outdoor table next to the hydrangeas at Logan Trading Company's Outboard Café, far away from the kitchen so Iris wouldn't have to smell the food cooking.

"Let's cut to the chase," Iris said. "I don't know how much longer I can last. We need to talk about promises. Number one," she said, "you're the kind of person everyone takes advantage of. Own it and get over it.

"Look," Iris said, pointing toward a lady in a nice silk shirt, her fingernails painted a perfect autumn red. "Good jewelry," she rasped.

Muriel looked. The woman had on a single, wide gold bracelet and a great pair of earrings, large pearls, with tiny sapphires crusting the gold setting.

"Would you ask that woman to bake cupcakes or pick up your child from school?"

"No," Muriel said.

"No one would, but they'd ask you. Promise me that from now on, you will always wear good jewelry and look just a little bitchy. I'm leaving you mother's pearls. They're good ones. She never wore them, and neither have I, but you must. You need them."

The first time Muriel wore the pearls was for Iris's funeral. They felt cool and heavy on her neck. When she touched them, rolling the large smooth beads between her fingers, she could hear in her mind the shussh-shussh sound of her college roommate praying the rosary every evening before she studied.

If she prayed when she touched the pearls, Muriel wondered, would Iris be able to hear her?

"I'd like to sit in that one," Muriel told the car salesman, pointing to a bright red sedan with a sunroof.

"Drive it?"

"No, just sit in it."

"Whatever," Mike said, unlocking the door. "I'll be over there if you want to take it for a test run."

Muriel pulled the door closed, rested her left hand on the wheel and touched her pearls with her right, then closed her eyes and tried to imagine Iris sitting next to her in the passenger seat.

"You said new things are always asking to be broken. I used to think it was an excuse you and mother made up as to why I should be happy to take your hand-me-downs."

Muriel punched the radio buttons, rolled the window down, and opened the glove compartment. She found an old AAA trip-tik to Boston and another to Florida.

"Been to Boston and made it back again. I didn't want your clothes. I wanted to be bold like you, but didn't know how."

Muriel tooted the horn and motioned for the salesman to come over. She liked the way the car felt. Liked the quick bitchy blare of the horn.

"So, are you with me, Iris? Want to take a spin?"

THE WITNESS

In my dream, I am suspended in the cool water of the ocean by a floatation device that fits comfortably under both of my arms, allowing my chin a sun-warmed place to rest. It looks like half of an inner tube that has been sewn shut on each end. It reminds me of the dunkers I used to buy at the campus snack shop, with the hopes that a donut and a black cup of coffee was all I needed to get me through a long night of studying, so many years ago in college when I was desperately failing Italian.

The rest of my body, my torso and legs, hang free in the water. I kick my feet and am effortlessly propelled forward. I am delighted the water isn't overly warm, and, in fact, is rather on the cool side. If it were too warm, it would make me sleepy and my progress would be just that much slower.

I was never a distance swimmer, only a sprinter, and a mediocre one at that.

My husband, Elliott, is a few feet ahead of me to my left. He has a full inner tube that he is alternately sitting in and hanging from. Occasionally, I see him take one long easy stroke with a free hand. The rest of the time, it seems as though he is gliding along with no effort at all. He seems to be enjoying the sun and the occasional breeze. Our son, Michael, is playing on a water mattress a few feet in front of us.

He is unaware of being carried along by the tide.

It has never occurred to me that it would be this easy to swim across the Atlantic Ocean.

"Irene," Elliott's hand touches my arm. I can hear him, but his voice seems very far away. "Irene, are you okay?"

He touches me again, this time stroking my head, brushing my hair away from my face. His touch is light, like a fresh spring breeze. I am reluctant, but at last willing to open my eyes.

"What time is it? Is Michael awake already? Did you tell me you had to go to the office early today?"

"You were trembling," Elliott says. "I didn't know if you were okay. I worried you might be sick or maybe you were just having a bad dream. I didn't want to wake you, but I wanted to be sure you were okay. You've been restless, tossing and turning, for the last hour."

His hand touches my forehead. He believes that all sickness is noted by fever. No fever, no sickness.

"I'm fine. I was dreaming that I, all of us, swam across the Atlantic Ocean."

"Sounds like a nightmare."

"Not really, it was easy. In fact, so easy, I couldn't understand why people haven't done it before, or why anyone would bother to fly. It was absolutely effortless. You were having a great time."

I want to go back to sleep. The dream was lovely. I want to fall back into it. I decide then and there that I must tell Miriam about the dream as soon as I get to work.

"What time is it?"

"Four o'clock."

Elliott yawns and raises his arm in the air like a teenager on the home stretch of a date, still hoping to catch a kiss or a hug.

"Want to give me a kiss?" he asks.

THE WITNESS

"Sure," I say, rolling over, "a kiss good night."

I close my eyes. The dream is still there. The three of us are still floating, still making our way from one shore to the other. I can see the harbor. We have less than a mile to go. I can't imagine how it can be this easy. I feel as though this is too good.

Just about the time I am willing to cast away my usual fears and abandon my natural skepticism for happy ever after, I see three boats: two gunners and a sailboat.

The dream is really a test. There is always a test. Isn't that the way it goes? I can see now that we are going to have to get through the gunners, past the sailboat in order to get to the shore alive.

Piece of cake. I get Elliott's attention. He grabs Michael's raft and the three of us head a mere hundred yards off our chartered course, slipping casually by the gunners and the sailboat as though they aren't even there.

As we get close, I am surprised to see steps at the shore. Michael tumbles off his raft, but within seconds I dive into the clear water and bring him laughing to the surface.

We are wet, but not tired. As we climb up the steps together to the shore, Elliott's uncle is waiting to take us to the hotel and give Michael his Easter basket.

"Weird dream," Elliott says the next morning.

"I rather liked the dream," I say.

"Swimming across the Atlantic Ocean seems like a pretty stressful situation. Maybe you're working too hard. Why not take today off?"

Elliott butters his second piece of toast, both sides, and then eyes me cautiously. He is the official interpreter of my dreams.

I disagree with him about his interpretation that I'm stressed out about my work, but I don't have time to say so because the phone rings. It's Don, Miriam's husband. He seems calm, but I can hear in his voice that he is struggling hard to maintain control. Miriam is my bookkeeper and she is missing.

"Have you called the police?" It is the only thing I can think of to ask. "Okay, don't worry. I know she's fine. I just have a feeling she is all right. I'll be in the office as soon as I get Michael to school. Call me when you know anything. Call if you just need to talk. If you want, we'll take Jason and Myra this evening. They're no trouble. We'll do whatever we can to help."

"Missing?" Elliott says before I can hang up the phone.

"Yes," I reply rather blankly. "She made a quick trip to the grocery store on Saturday evening to pick up a few things for dinner and she never came back. They found her car in the parking lot, but that's all. No identification. No sign of struggle. No witnesses. No hint of foul play. Nothing."

"Nothing?"

"As far as Don knows, she just disappeared."

"People don't just disappear."

"I need to get to the office. The police will be there shortly. They want to look around, see if there's any note, any hint of what might have happened or where she might have gone."

I close my eyes. I feel oddly calm. I can't explain why, but I know Miriam is okay. I can feel it wash over me like a warm wave.

"Do you think my dream was about Miriam?" I ask Elliott.

"That Miriam drowned?"

"No, that maybe she just swam away."

"Do you think she just walked off?" Elliott asks.

"I guess I'd rather believe she walked away than she was kidnapped, beaten, raped or killed."

My hands are numb.

THE WITNESS

I am trying to get Michael out of his car seat and am having trouble unbuckling him. He is patient and chatters on about Kelly, his friend at the daycare. He is trying to tell me something about Kelly, but as hard as I try to listen, I can't, so I simply agree and let him chatter on happily.

When I get back to my car, after dropping Michael off at daycare, I fumble with the keys. It's already 9:30 a.m.. I don't want the police to get to the office before I do. I have a ten o'clock with the sales rep from Jantzen. The new spring line of cotton sweaters has to be looked at and decisions have to be made.

It isn't even the middle of January, and already I'm getting worried about Easter. Both Christmas and after-Christmas sales were slow and I've got to think seriously about how much merchandise we can realistically move in the next season.

Safely inside my car, my key slips into the ignition. The car responds. Once again, the moment feels easy.

I swam across the ocean last night. I'm pretty sure I can make it through the day.

"Did she talk to you much about things that bothered her?"

The policeman is a detective and he is talking to me while his eyes are scanning the room, looking at my desk, the curtains, the Sierra Club Calendar nailed to the back of our office door. While he looks and asks questions, he scribbles down my answers in a ratty notebook.

"Stop," I almost shout at him.

"Stop what?" he replies.

"Stop looking around the room when you ask me questions."

His looking around while he takes notes makes me nervous, makes me think there are things in the room, clues to Miriam's unhappiness I failed to notice before. What did I miss?

"I'm sorry, bad habit," he says, flipping his notebook closed for the moment. He shifts in his chair, leans back comfortably then starts again.

"Did she confide in you?"

"Miriam has worked with me ever since I opened the store. She was the first employee I ever hired. We shared an office. We talked. I knew her family. She told me things, but nothing that would indicate anything like this."

"Like what?" he asks, opening his notebook again. He leans forward in his chair as though we are about to share a confidence. I do not like him.

"Like disappearing," I say.

"Who said she disappeared?"

"She's not here, is she?"

Disappeared is easier to say than a word like dead or something stupid like she passed away or went to be with God, as though she and God might be out having lunch together somewhere and as soon as she's done visiting, she'll come back.

I want this man to leave.

"No," he says, smiling a little, "she's not here. Do you know where she is?"

"No."

"She was your bookkeeper?" he asks.

He leans back in his chair again and begins to take more notes.

"Yes, for the last eight years."

"She must have been pregnant then, eight years ago, with her first child."

"Yes, with Myra, her daughter."

"And you weren't afraid to hire someone who was pregnant?"

"Pregnant women are not usually known to be dangerous," I say.

"Sure," he says, with a little too much of a smile, "but they're not considered that stable. I mean, as workers, you know. They need time off for sick children and all that parenting stuff."

I feel myself getting angry. I want this man gone from my office. I want him to leave Miriam alone, even though she isn't here and I don't know where she is right now. For sure, I don't want someone like him tracking her down and dragging her home.

"Miriam is never late for work. When she has appointments or 'parenting' things she needs to attend to, she does, but she uses her own sick leave for that time. She is a good mother, and from what I can tell, a devoted wife. She has taken care of all of my bookkeeping for the last eight years and there has never been a penny missing or a check or bank balance amiss."

He hasn't written down a word of what I just said. He closes his notebook again.

"We're going to have to take your books for the time being for evidence," he tells me as he begins to clear the top of Miriam's desk, stuffing everything into a large plastic bag he has pulled from his jacket pocket. "Everything will be copied then returned to you. We'll also need her time cards and pay records."

"We don't keep time cards."

"You must have some record of her work attendance."

"I have schedule sheets."

"We'll need to see those."

"Is there anything else?" I ask, an edge creeping into my voice. I push my chair back as though I am dismissing a freshly disciplined child from my office.

"I suspect this is hard," he says.

I know he is trying to apologize, but I don't want to hear what he has to say. I turn away from him and begin fiddling with the Jantzen files on my desk.

"I know she was a friend as well as an employee," he continues softly. "You need to know we have found no evidence of foul play. There have been no witnesses come forward. Her husband doesn't seem to know anything or give any clues as to if or why she would just walk out on him and their family. She seems to have few close friends. We don't see this often, maybe once or twice a year, and only with women, but sometimes people just get up and walk away. Sometimes they know what they are doing, and sometimes they just wander off and eventually get themselves lost or hurt.

"She might have been abducted, but the signs aren't there. For what it's worth, I have a feeling about this one. I think she walked away. I hope to God she hasn't been hurt. I hope she made a safe clean break for herself. I don't really care about the reasons she might have had for leaving, except that those reasons might give us some clue as to where she went and whether or not she's safe."

"Thanks," I say.

"Do you have any reason to believe she wanted to leave her husband? Any talk about another man? Any signs of depression? Anything that might be suspicious or give you reason to think she was unhappy?"

I am so tired. I think about swimming across the ocean last night and wonder if I feel tired because I swam so far before getting here today.

The sales rep is going to arrive in ten minutes and I am going to have to make some decisions about our spring inventory.

I know the detective wants some kind of answer. That he is going to insist I tell him something prophetic, something he can hold onto like an inner tube: something to help him float.

I try hard to think about Miriam: Miriam laughing; Miriam

worrying about taxes, store sales, flu shots, and her son's slight stammer; Miriam staying late the night of her tenth anniversary, trying on every dress in the store, hoping to find something perfect to wear for dinner with her husband because she knew Alan had bought her a diamond ring, the one thing she wanted but they couldn't afford ten years ago when they first got married.

Miriam in a pale yellow dress with a soft white jacket. Miriam fighting with the buyers because merchandise we ordered and paid for didn't arrive on time. Miriam, my friend, the one I used to tell all my troubles to.

"I'm sorry," I say. My throat is dry and tight. "There's nothing I can think of. No man. No troubles I know of. No talk ever about leaving, or problems. I can't think of anything."

"There must be something," the detective says, looking at his notebook again. "Anything. Did she ever talk about things that upset her?"

Three minutes to ten. The clock is ticking in my head.

"She hated capital punishment," I offer.

"What do you mean?" he says, writing it down.

"You know, capital punishment, the electric chair, executions. She hated executions. She wouldn't read the papers when there was a story about an upcoming execution. Would turn off the radio if they started talking about it. She didn't want her children to know about them. She had a real thing about executions."

"Any reason you can think of why?" he asks.

"Why what?"

"Why she hated them so much?" he says, picking up the papers he has collected from her desk. He buttons his coat.

"I guess," I start to say, then stop because the detective has begun walking away from me. "Because," I go on, a little louder, hoping to make him stop and listen, "she thought it was a waste of human life, that it was inhumane. That maybe no one should willfully, righteously kill anyone. That maybe the people who were being executed might be innocent. That maybe it's just wrong to destroy a life."

"I'll have someone from the station bring these back to you sometime tomorrow. I hope it won't be too much of an inconvenience. In the meantime, if you think of anything, call. Here's my card."

My office door closes and he is gone. I look up at the clock. The sales rep is late.

If Miriam were here now, I'd close the door and tell her about my dream. About how easy it was to swim across the ocean last night and how refreshing the water felt. She would listen intently and maybe even laugh a little. Eventually, she would ask what Elliott thought the dream meant.

I would tell her, and probably she would laugh again and disagree. Maybe she would tell me that the dream wasn't about working hard at all. Most likely, she would say the dream was a good one. That it was a sign that we should buy more swimsuits because the spring line would be hot this year and would sell out before the first of May.

After we finished interpreting my dream, we would start talking about what to order. The phone would ring and I would never get around to asking her if she ever dreamt about swimming across the ocean.

Everything felt so easy and perfect in my dream last night. I close my eyes and try to capture that feeling again. I try to picture Miriam sitting across from me at her desk. I try to see her face, read it like a treasure map: try to discover if she is swimming or drowning.

I imagine her being in the room with me. Her face is smooth. She is smiling. It is a smile that looks easy, not forced. It is a smile that can mean anything. It could be asking for help or just saying hello.

THE WITNESS

I blink my eyes and she is gone.

I wonder if it would be easy for me to drive to the store, get out of my car, and walk away from everything.

I look over at Miriam's desk again, and see her favorite dark blue sweater draped across the back of her chair. On her desk are pictures of her kids and an assortment of note pads and an old coffee cup full of neatly sharpened pencils.

Miriam always did her bookkeeping in pencil rather than in ink because she believed it was all too easy to make a mistake.

I pick up the card the detective gave me. I dial his number. I want to tell him one more thing.

I get his answer machine and wait for the beep.

"Miriam believed anyone could make a mistake," I say, gathering my thoughts to make sense of what has happened, "and that everyone deserves a second chance."

BLACK TIE OPTIONAL

Jeanette was not pleased to see a note sticking out from underneath her apartment door. Even before she picked it up she knew it was from Sonia, who called herself Sonny, and that it was more than likely about Sonia's teenage son.

Sonny lived in the apartment down the hall with her nutso-hyper son, Kevin. Sonny had never mentioned an ex-husband or, for that matter, that Kevin actually had a father, so Jeanette always figured Sonny was either gay or extremely angry about some one-night stand. In either case, Sonny spent most of her time looking for help with Kevin, and Jeanette did her best not to be available.

"No," Jeanette said with resolve, "no, no, and no."

She pulled the note out from under the door with the toe of her shoe. There, just as she had feared, was Sonny's wild scrawling handwriting galloping across the back of a used envelope: "I'm desperate. Have to work late tonight. Could you take Kevin to his concert at school? He needs to be there by 5:30. Blessings. Sonny."

"Whoa, wait a minute, sister," Jeanette murmured as she reread the note. She did not have plans for the evening, but if she did, they for sure, by Jupiter, would not involve the likes of Kevin. Jeanette had been very careful to make it crystal clear to Sonny that she didn't do kids, especially wacko kids like Kevin who never shut up.

BLACK TIE OPTIONAL

Jeanette didn't make a big deal about it but made sure Sonny understood that if she had wanted to spend time with a kid she would have had one of own. In fact, still single and childless at forty-two, she had pretty much resolved she was going to be alone the rest of her life, and she liked it that way. Being involved with someone always made her life more complicated.

She didn't like complicated. She liked easy. Truth was, she didn't really like children. She liked quiet. She liked order. She liked sleeping late and watching R-rated movies. She despised everything Walt Disney had ever touched.

Thump. Thump. Thump. Kevin was jumping up the back staircase. He always jumped up the stairs as though he was in training for the Olympics. He never climbed the stairs quietly the way a normal person would do. It was one of Kevin's many annoying habits.

Before Jeanette could cram the note into her pocket and jam her key into the lock so she could get inside and fake not being there, Kevin was standing in front of her. He had his clarinet case in one hand and a rather ratty black tie that was far too thin to be fashionable in his other. Jeanette guessed Sonny had gotten it at the Goodwill.

"My mother forgot to tie this for me," Kevin said, pushing the narrow satin tie toward Jeanette. "She usually ties it then slips it over the shirt collar so all I have to do is button the shirt, then pull the tie up after I slip the whole mess over my head. But she forgot and I don't know how to do it and I've already been to see Mr. Marcuso on the first floor and he told me that he was a postman not an executive and that the only tie he ever wore was to his first communion forty years ago and that he didn't tie his own tie then and he couldn't tie this one for me now. Could you do it?"

"How old are you?" Jeanette snapped. It was a rhetorical question, the edge of which, she hoped, would not be lost on Kevin. She hoped, in fact, that her sarcasm would stop him cold. She was wrong.

"I'm fourteen and seven twelfths," Kevin said precisely. His unshakable need to be both exact and truthful was another one of his annoying habits. "But, I'm short. My mother is not short. She's 5' 8 1/2", which is tall for a woman. But, I'm only 5' 5" and that makes me short. I think I'm the shortest boy in the high school. We have to get going. I have to be there by 5:30. Actually, I think I need to be there by 5:15 but I told my mother 5:30 because I thought if I said 5:30 she'd be able to take me. But I guess she can't and it's almost five now which means if we don't hurry I'm going to be late. The lowest band always plays first so it's really important I get there on time. If I'm late for one more thing, Mr. Hunter, the band teacher, is going to take 10 points off my grade. My grade isn't that good to begin with, so 10 points is a lot for me to lose."

Jeanette suppressed the urge to run into her apartment so she could slam the door in Kevin's face.

"Any chance in Hell that you even know how to get to your school?" Jeanette asked coolly, because she knew, despite the fact that she didn't want to, she was going to take Kevin to his concert.

"I know the bus route. But, my guess is that the bus route is not the best or the quickest way to get there. Once we turn up Foster Avenue it's maybe four or six blocks."

"Which is it? Four or six? Makes a difference."

"I'll be able to tell you once we get on Foster. I'll know for sure then. Mom says I'm a visual learner, someone who needs visual cues to help them get the answer. That's why I'm always drawing pictures. If they let me draw pictures in school instead of taking notes, I'd be the smartest person in the class. That's what my mom says. But they don't let you draw pictures in high school. My teacher calls it daydreaming and doodling, and it seems like there's some kind of law against daydreaming and doodling once you hit high school. I've gotten into a lot of trouble over the issue."

"I bet you have. What's the name of your school?"

"St Raphael's."

"You're Catholic?" Jeanette asked, as she moved down the hallway in the hopes of getting this little job of driving Kevin to school over with quickly.

Kevin trailed obediently behind her.

"Jewish, but my mom says a Catholic school is better for me because the kids aren't as smart. I have this learning thing. It's hard for me to focus. Also, I'm not so good at writing. My mom says I can talk a blue streak but when I start to try to put words on paper things get a bit jumbled and backwards. I'm in ninth grade, but I'm still trying to pass the eighth grade-writing test. Even though I flunked the test last year, they let me go on. I guess they can do what they want at Catholic schools, which is another reason Mom says they're better for me than the public schools. If I were in public school I'd probably spend ten years in eighth grade. I took the test three times last year and flunked it every time. Sister Matthews said she'd make a special test for me. It's not really a test, but a book report. I've already read the book, *Animal Farm*. I thought I understood it and wrote about the animals but I guess I flunked that paper too. Sister Matthews is working with me now after school on Thursdays. She says *Animal Farm* is an allegory. She got kind of angry that I hadn't figured it out on my own. She says it's really not about the animals but about politics and the world. I didn't get that, but if Sister Matthews says it's true, I guess it's true. If I don't pass the test by the end of the year, I'm going to have to repeat ninth grade. I really don't want to do that."

"Listen, …"

"It's too late for me to take the bus. My mom is in some meeting and I can't reach her. Mr. Hunter will kill me. Can you just try to fix my tie?"

"No." Jeanette said firmly. "I'll take you to the school, but that's it."

She pushed opened the door in order to go outside. Kevin followed her.

Jeanette's car was parked in the perfect space, right in front of the building. She knew, as sure as she knew Kevin wouldn't shut up, that when she came back, that good space would be gone and she'd be walking two blocks or more back to her apartment in the cold.

"My father left my mother when I was two weeks old so I don't know if he wears a tie or not. He didn't even come to my Bar Mitzvah. My mother gave me his phone number on my thirteenth birthday and I called him. I thought if I talked to him he might like me and might want to see me read from the Torah. He's Jewish. Did your father wear a tie?"

"Maybe Mr. Hunter can tie it for you," Jeanette snapped.

"Apparently you've never met Mr. Hunter. He hates me. Says I should give up the clarinet and get out of his life. I love the clarinet. I can play ten songs and all the scales in the beginning book. I wish I could take private lessons, but Mom says we can't afford them. I'm in the lowest band. But I don't care. Sitting there in the middle of the music is so amazing. You can't hear anything else in the world, nothing but the music. Sometimes I sit so still when I'm playing that I can feel my heart beat. Woody Allen plays clarinet. He's Jewish too. Will you help me with my tie?"

"Have one of your friends tie it," Jeanette said as she opened the door of her car and pushed the button to unlock the other doors. She toyed with the idea of asking Kevin to sit in the backseat but thought that if she did that he would probably slide on over behind her and start jabbering in her ear.

"I have a reputation for being a crybaby. Crybabies don't have friends. Are you going to stay and hear me play? I'm scared my mom won't make it. And when I get scared I kind of lose it and I talk too much. I have this crazy idea that if I just keep talking, nothing bad will happen. Sometimes my mom doesn't do what she says she's going to do, like show up at my concerts or pick me up. She's always sorry when it happens. But, it's like me being a crybaby. It happens. I know it happens and it could happen again tonight. Catholic parents come to everything. I mean EVERYTHING. Mr. Hunter had to bring me home after the last concert because my mom didn't come to pick me up. That's when he told me I should give up the clarinet."

"I said I'd take you to your school. I didn't say anything about staying to hear you play."

Kevin slid into the passenger seat, buckled his seat belt and closed his car door.

"Thank you, for taking me to school." he said, slowly, closing his eyes and rubbing the flat smooth end of the ratty black tie against his cheek.

"Stop that," Jeanette yelled, grabbing the tie.

"What?"

"Fourteen-year-olds don't do things like that."

"You're right. I'm fourteen, nearly fifteen, and fourteen-year-olds don't do things like rubbing the end of a tie against their face. My mother is always telling me to stop and think before I do things. Stop and think. Stop and think. She told me you didn't like kids, that maybe you had trouble with kids or trouble having kids, but that in any case I needed to stop and think before I said or did anything around you and that I should say thank you. I didn't think. That's all. I didn't think. I'm sorry you didn't have any children."

"I never wanted kids," Jeanette said, handing him back the tie. "There's no sorry about it. Just don't do that with the tie. It's a crybaby thing. Okay?"

"Okay. I don't remember if I thanked you already. So, in case I didn't, thank you. Thank you very much. I know some people find me annoying. Mr. Marcuso says I'm the most annoying person he's ever met and tells me to quit bothering him. You never say that to me. You're very nice. Thank you."

"Where's your school?" Jeanette asked as she turned down Foster Avenue.

Kevin leaned forward and looked out the windshield. When he didn't see his school, he leaned back in order to look out the side window again.

"I guess it was six blocks, not four, maybe even eight. Could you go just a little further? The bus always turns down Foster. There," he says pointing to a line of cars parked along the curb by the school. "I told you Catholic parents come to everything. I hate it. I mean, I really hate it. I bet your parents came to everything, didn't they?"

"No."

"Don't lie to me! I hate it when people lie to me."

Kevin unbuckled his belt as though he was going to leap from the car before Jeanette could pull over and stop.

"Let me take you to the door," Jeanette offered.

"No," Kevin shouted, "I mean, no, please, don't take me to the door. It's better if I walk. Stop the car. Please, stop the car!"

Jeanette stopped the car and before she could say anything else, Kevin opened the door, jumped out and began running towards the school. His clarinet was tucked under his arm like a football and his white shirt, which was too big for him, had come undone in the back and was billowing out like a torn sail as he ran down the sidewalk to the school. Jeanette watched him as he ran.

The car behind her blew its horn. She turned on her blinker and as she did she looked over on the seat and saw the tie. Kevin had left his tie.

"Kevin," she called out, even though she knew he could not hear her. She picked up his tie and before she could stop what she was doing, she pressed it against her cheek. It felt soft and cool like a child's hand. She eased her car out into the tangle of parents looking for parking places. She saw an empty space about a half a block away on the right. She looked at her watch. It was almost 5:30. She slid into the parking spot.

When she got into the school she didn't know exactly where to go or what she was going to do, so she just followed the flow of parents and as she walked, she looked for Mr. Hunter.

"Kevin's tie," she called out to a tall heavyset man she assumed was Mr. Hunter. He was standing outside the auditorium, holding a baton. He turned to look at her.

"I forgot to give Kevin his tie."

"Kevin's in the lowest band," Mr. Hunter said, as though this would be news to her, something else she had obviously failed to grasp about Kevin's shortcomings.

"Yes, I know," she said, holding out the tie, "he forgot his tie."

"The black tie is optional for the lowest group. Only the symphonic band, the top group, has to wear them. Kevin knows that."

"He loves the clarinet," she said, again offering him the tie. "He doesn't care that he's in the lowest group."

"You're not his mother, are you?"

"No."

"Lucky you," Mr. Hunter said taking hold of the end of the tie in order to pull it free from her hand.

Jeanette held tight to the tie, forcing Mr. Hunter to struggle with her for a moment.

"He can play ten songs and all the scales in the beginning book," she said, a little louder and more defensively than she had intended. Then she let go of the tie, and when she did Mr. Hunter was thrown off balance and had to take a quick step back in order to keep from falling.

"I don't know anything about ties," she said, "and Kevin's father is a real jerk so consequently, the kid needs a little help in the tie department. It's important that he gets to wear the tie. Real important."

"Sure," Mr. Hunter said, looking first at her then back at the tie in his hand. "I'll give it to him."

"And tie it for him," she added. "He needs someone to tie it for him."

HOPSCOTCH

June flipped up her coat collar and tightened the woolen scarf around her neck in order to protect herself from the morning chill. She was on early border patrol. The work was dirty: reporting people who crossed illegally from Mexico to the US so the border agents could hunt them down. She hated the whole idea of it but did what she could, when she could, to throw a wrench into the system. She had had to fight hard and eventually leave everything behind in order to escape an abusive marriage. She knew just how desperate someone would have to be to take a chance on the river to find a better life on the other side.

She pulled on her work gloves and dragged the chain that was wrapped around two spare tires and secured it to the right side of the bumper of her truck. Once she felt it wouldn't pull lose if she ran over a tree limb or snagged a rock, she grabbed the second chain and attached the other two tires to the left side of the bumper. She readied the tires, kicking them into place. The sun was just beginning to come up, lighting a soft orange line along the banks of the Rio Grande and threatening to melt the bits of frozen dew here and there on the edge of the riverbank.

"Need help?" her boss Grady called out from the open window of his pickup. He'd pulled over to the side of the road and was just sitting there watching June struggle with the tires.

"Not from you," June called back, not bothering to wave. Grady got on her nerves the way he was always hovering around like he was king of something wonderful and had to make sure everyone followed his rules. As if rules and borders were the only things that kept the world safe.

It had been eleven days since she'd reported seeing any footprints. It was the longest stretch of no reports she'd dared so far. Grady had called her out on it yesterday when she got back and filed her report, but she shrugged it off, saying she guessed it had just been too damn cold lately for anyone to swim across the Rio Grande. She knew Grady would be watching her today.

"You take a good look now, while you're out there this morning," Grady said, gunning his engine. "A real good look. That's why we're paying you, in case you've forgot."

"Like some criminal would wade across this damn river on a cold night just to have the privilege of robbing your ugly house," June said giving a yank on the second chain to be sure it wouldn't come lose when she was dragging the tires through the sand.

God, she hated Grady and his smug self and she hated this job. But there wasn't much else to do in town except work at the Wal-Mart, and she simply didn't have the patience for stocking shelves or helping people find applesauce on aisle three.

Just the other day when she was buying groceries, some lady had pushed her cart right next to June's and asked what the difference was between jam and jelly, as if June was already wearing a badge that said she worked there.

Grady slowly pulled his truck forward a few feet, stopped, backed up, spun his tires just to show off and leaned out the window again.

"What makes you think these people won't want to come knocking on your door to rob you?"

HOPSCOTCH

June ignored him and pulled the four tires into place, one next to the other to form a snug dragline.

"Or worse, yet, rape you? In case you were wondering, that's why we do this job, to protect ourselves against people like them."

June walked around to the driver's side of her truck, reached in and turned on the ignition. She put her left foot on the running board and gave herself a boost up so she could look out over the cab at Grady.

"What's the difference between jelly and jam?" she yelled out over the hum of her engine.

"Shoot..." Grady said, popping his truck into first gear and spinning the tires again on the frozen gravel as he jumped back onto the pavement of the road. "You better take a good, hard look today. That's your job, and you better do it right if you want to keep it."

"Like I care," June called out to the dust on the road. She slid into the driver's seat and slammed her door. She flipped on her high beams, put the truck into low gear and began inching her way along the riverbank, dragging the tires behind her.

The sun had warmed the sand just enough to make the sweep easier. She glanced in her rearview mirror in order to check out the smooth surface the tires she was dragging had made in her wake. She was paid to make two sweeps a day over the twenty miles of her route along the river: one just at the edge of the water, the second touching the smooth surface of the top line of the first pass of the drag line on her return. Two sweeps, as though anyone who had swum across the Rio Grande in the middle of the night might have the strength to jump nearly fifteen feet in order to scramble up the grassy bank beyond. She took a sip of hot coffee from her thermos.

She'd drive the twenty miles there and back, forty miles total at her usual five miles an hour, letting her eyes glide from side to side to check the sand for prints. She took her time. Four hours up and four hours back. She was only paid for six, but she took the eight. She didn't have anything else to do and she enjoyed the solitude. Plus, it just about drove Grady crazy that she took so long to do the route: crazy enough that he left her alone most days.

Grady had followed her once or twice recently. She worried he was getting suspicious about her recent lack of crossing reports, but on the other hand, she was certain she had nothing to worry about. It was too cold for him to get out of his truck.

He had slowed down a bit yesterday while she was driving her route and had stayed at the edge of the road, creeping along to follow her, just to get on her nerves.

She did a good job of ignoring him the whole time he followed her. Never even turned her head to acknowledge he was there. She just kept moving forward as slowly as she could, knowing that Grady was too lazy to leave the warmth of his truck and walk down the embankment to check on her.

So far this morning, she hadn't seen anything. As awful as the whole border patrol mess was, she knew she needed to find something to report today. Eleven straight days with no prints wouldn't go unnoticed by people higher than Grady, cold river or not.

Her truck heater made a rattling whirring noise. June banged on the dashboard with her fist, trying to encourage the heater to keep working. If the heater went out now, she'd be frozen stiff before she got back and unhitched the tires from her bumper. She took another sip of her hot coffee.

She rocked her right foot forward and pushed on the accelerator, inching the speedometer up to ten miles an hour. She needed to get to the end of her route so she could turn off the truck and add some antifreeze. God, it was cold.

HOPSCOTCH

Her truck rolled smoothly along the edge of the riverbank. The tires dug into the wet sand, creating a smooth fresh surface. She turned on the wipers and hiked up the blower on her dead heater hoping that some of the fog that was collecting along the bottom of her windshield would clear. She let her eyes sweep back and forth to the slow rhythm of the wipers. That's when she saw the two small sets of prints.

She slowed down, tapping the brakes, glancing up at the road to check for Grady before she came to a stop. A beat-up mini van whizzed by on the road. June waited until she couldn't see or hear it. She checked in her rearview mirror. She hadn't seen Grady since she'd left and wondered where he might be.

She knew Grady was having an affair with Rhonda, a friend of hers who lived right up the road near the end of her route. Rhonda had shared a beer with June a couple months ago and told her all about it. Said Grady wasn't much of a lover, but he was married, so she had her nights free. When June had asked Rhonda why she even bothered, she'd said something lame like you might as well sleep with the one you're with rather than the one you want. Whatever that meant.

More than once lately, June had seen Grady's truck cruise by on the way to Rhonda's, slowing just enough to make it look like he was on official business.

She reached under the seat and grabbed the jug of antifreeze. She thought she'd turn off the truck, let it cool like she had planned and use the antifreeze as an excuse for why she stopped if Grady happened to drive by on his way to see Rhonda.

Once out of the truck June could more carefully examine the two sets of prints. One was long and narrow like they might belong to a woman. The other set was small enough to be those of a six-, maybe seven-year-old child. Both looked like the prints of cheap flat sandals: flip-flops, or maybe even house slippers.

About five steps in, she saw the first barefoot print.

It was the smaller of the two sets. June bent down and pressed her hand into the tiny bare print wondering if it was still warm. The wind, skidding across the cold water of the Rio Grande, sent a chill up her back. She could see how the big toe of the little foot had dug into the sand as though it were trying to get some purchase. Barefoot. She pulled up her collar and sent up a quick prayer. She looked around and saw the abandoned sandal blown up against a clump of weeds. She picked it up and shoved it into her jacket pocket. She hoped the child who had lost the shoe was still alive.

She stood up and looked down the road before turning back to her truck. It was about that time of day when Grady made his love run. She popped the hood and unscrewed the lid on the antifreeze. She needed to make it look like she could take care of herself. Not give Grady any reason to stop and help. As she poured the antifreeze, she let her eyes follow the footprints across the sand until they disappeared in the grassy embankment. The larger of the two sets of prints moved step-by -step, one foot in front of the other. Tired. Cold. Determined.

Halfway across the sandy bank, the smaller steps changed rhythm. The foot with the shoe, coming down deep and solo. The bare foot landing a few inches later in tandem with the other. Over and over in a pattern: One foot solo, two feet together, one foot solo, two feet together.

"Hopscotch," June said under her breath.

The tracks were faint. The wintry wind had already blown some trace of the two people away. You'd have to be close to see for sure they were human footprints. If it had rained during the night, the prints would have been washed away completely and she wouldn't have had to worry about them. June guessed by the size of both sets of prints that it was a young mother with her child. But it could also be two sisters or cousins. June had heard that families often sent their daughters out on their own with the hopes they'd make it across and be allowed to stay.

About three feet before the sand quit, where there was grass and windblown trash that would hide their crossing, the hopscotch prints disappeared, as though the older one had picked up the smaller child and run.

She heard a truck approach and slow down. She looked up. It was Grady.

"Need help?" Grady called out as he pulled to the side of the road.

"Nah," June responded, holding up the bottle of antifreeze for Grady to see. "Too cold for my old truck. Just adding some antifreeze to help it along."

"See anything?"

"An old minivan cruised by about half an hour ago."

"Any footprints?"

"Who'd be desperate enough to swim across this damn river last night? Any colder and they would have had to break ice."

"You sure you haven't seen any footprints?"

"You want me to back up and try again?"

"Just want you to do what you're getting paid to do."

"Did you figure it out yet?" June called up to Grady's truck. She could hear Grady tapping on the accelerator, revving his engine impatiently. Heat was probably pouring out of the window as he ran his mouth and gunned his engine. He wasn't even wearing gloves or a hat.

"What?" he growled.

"The difference between jelly and jam?" June said, capping the antifreeze and slamming her truck hood shut.

"Just do your job and don't mess up," Grady yelled out before he rolled up his window and drove off in Rhonda's direction.

June got into her truck and turned the ignition. She let the engine warm just enough to keep it from conking out. While she waited for the truck to settle down, she looked up the road to be sure Grady wasn't circling back to check on her. When she was sure she was safe, she eased up on the clutch and let the truck roll forward, waiting for the tug of the chains to pull the tires across the sand. She stayed in low gear, rolling just barely five miles an hour.

She gripped the steering wheel with her left hand and turned to look over her right shoulder so she could use the back of her gloved hand to clear the fog off the rear window of her truck.

She wanted to be sure the drag tires smoothed the sand. They did what they were meant to do. The prints were gone.

She checked her watch. She had a little less than thirty-five minutes before Grady would double back down the road. If he wasn't much, like Rhonda said, at least he was quick. Some women would put up with anything.

June had three more miles to go before the twenty-mile mark. Three miles there and three back to deal with the rest of the footprints. Six miles all together to take care of business. She was pretty sure Grady was tucking into Rhonda's bed about now. She let the weight of her boot bear down on the pedal, pushing the truck to ten, then fifteen miles an hour, slow enough that the drag of the tires would continue to bite into the sand.

As soon as she had cleared the first set of tracks, she pushed the truck a little harder, edging close to 20 miles an hour. She did the math in her head: at 20 miles an hour she could get to the end and back to erase the second set of footprints in less than 20 minutes. That is, unless there were others who had crossed last night.

"Please God," June whispered under her breath. She needed to find some other footprints or better yet, a whole group of footprints. Big ones, men who could run fast, could already be lost and hard to find. If she didn't report something, she worried she'd lose her job.

In the meantime, she needed to get rid of the two remaining smaller sets of prints before Grady saw them. June gripped the steering wheel with both hands and slid forward in her seat so she could look out over the dashboard. Her eyes made a quick sweep both back and forth and forward a bit. If she discovered other tracks, she'd have to slow down in plenty of time without slamming on her brakes, to be sure the drag tires didn't get tangled up. She'd have to count them, make a guess of how many had crossed last night and whether they were male or female. Maybe she'd only report some of the tracks, not all of them: just enough to get Grady off her back for a few more days.

She could see the twenty-mile mark ahead of her. Nothing. There had only been the two people last night that had made it across.

She drove past the twenty-mile marker and eased her truck around to make the second sweep. She left the truck running as she jumped out to reposition the tires side-by-side in a neat row. She jumped back into the shelter of her truck and pushed her report sheet aside.

She checked her watch. If Grady was as quick as Rhonda said he was, she had about twelve minutes to make the double back before he'd come along to check on her again.

June slowed down as she approached the footprints. The wind had shifted a little since she had passed and had blown more sand, filling the soft shallow indentations the small feet had made. The clearest print left was the single one in the hopscotch pattern, the weight of the child landing sure on one foot, making it clear he or she had been there.

Grady's truck approached. When June heard his tires bite into the gravel at the side of the road and roll to a stop, she kept moving forward watching in her rearview mirror as the drag tires erased the last of the hopscotch game.

The wind blew, picking up bits of loose sand kicked up by the tires. She waved at Grady, signaling that there was nothing to report. He honked his horn and drove off.

She took her time getting back.

SIX

"Six," the doctor says.

I blink and he says it again.

"If you don't want to do anything you have six..."

"Days?" I ask.

The word leapt out before I could catch it or call it back.

"No one really knows," he apologizes.

I unzip my purse and pull out my calendar. I begin flipping the pages, wondering what I should reschedule. Cancel.

"Weeks?" I offer.

The doctor looks at my file on his desk.

I wonder if I should I get one more haircut.

"Months?" I say, shuffling through my calendar, counting the weeks/months to December 25th. Today is June 15th. Thanksgiving remains a remote possibility. Christmas would be a stretch.

"Maybe, but not years." The corners of his mouth twitch. It isn't exactly a smile. He shakes his head a little.

"Am I making you uncomfortable?" I ask, carefully tearing out the last two weeks of December.

"I'm guessing that you're not going to do anything," he says, making a note in my file.

Six days. Six weeks. Six months.

666: The Mark of the Devil.

"What would you do?" I ask, handing him the pages I have just torn out of my date book.

He pulls his trashcan from beneath his desk and throws the pages away.

I look at him.

He looks at me. He picks up a pencil from his desk and starts rolling it between his hands, clicking it across his wedding ring like a metronome, back and forth, click, click, click, click. It's a little like listening to a faucet drip.

"Do you have family?" he asks.

"Parents are dead, no husband."

"Children?"

How good or bad would it be if I lied six days, six weeks, or even six months before dying? I don't answer his question.

"What would you do?" I ask again.

"I would have to think about it," he says. "It's not an easy question."

"No shit," I say.

"The treatments are tough and I'm not sure they would buy you more than a couple of weeks at best. Plus you always risk the chance of complications."

"I'm hearing a no. Is that what I'm hearing? That you wouldn't take any treatments? That you'd just go peacefully into that dark night? That you'd empty your bank account and go to Paris."

"You know someone in Paris?" he asks.

"That bit about Paris was rhetorical, you know, like… take the last few days of your life and live it up. Drink some once in a lifetime expensive French wine, work through your bucket list."

"What a stupid movie," he says leaning back in his chair as though

SIX

he is trying to find the courage to fall backwards out of an airplane, rip cord in hand.

"You didn't like the movie?" I ask.

"All everyone wants to know now is whether or not they should work through their bucket list or take the treatments. Do I look like a fortune teller?"

"And, what do you say to them?"

"What would you?"

"You're the doctor. You're supposed to know. What is it? Six days, six weeks, six months? You've already told me it isn't six years."

"There are miracles," he says, looking up at the ceiling.

"I'm not feeling it," I tell him. "I'm feeling like the truth would be a good thing, much better than a miracle. I'm guessing miracles are miracles because they don't happen to everyone, just special people, and right now I'm not feeling very special."

"Medicine is not the exact science everyone wants it to be," he says, like I forgot to read the assignment before I got to class.

I try my damnedest to stare right through him, to make him as uncomfortable as I can...uncomfortable enough to quit waltzing around and get to the truth.

"Six months would be a gift," he says. "Something between six weeks and six months is my guess."

"Thanks for putting yourself out there," I say.

"This isn't easy for me either," he says.

"Say you've got a little less than six months to live, and could maybe get a couple more weeks if you took some truly, in the righteous sense of the word, killer drugs, would you take them?" I ask.

"The truth?" he asks, looking at the ceiling again.

"Nothing but..."

"I'd go to Paris."

As I leave his office, I dog-ear and rip off the corners of six month's worth of pages in my week-at-a-glance calendar. Walking from the office to my car, I drop the tiny corners from my fingers like breadcrumbs, leaving a trail. Marking my exit. I don't plan to come back.

I drive to my favorite coffee shop, order a blended latte, and ask for a double shot of whipped cream. Why not? I take a comfortable seat near the corner. Alone.

I don't mind being alone. Never have. I pull a blank 3x5 card from my purse and start making a list.

My life has been a series of lists. I made my first list in third grade, mapping out my plan to go to college. It was a simple list, but it had a goal and some clear objectives: study hard, make good grades, go to high school and make good grades, get into college. Study hard, get good grades, graduate, go somewhere wonderful and get a job.

I had a plan, even if, in the end, my parents refused to help me.

I like having plans, connecting the dots, going forward with my list in hand. I rarely get discouraged. Just make a new list when things fall apart.

They've fallen apart.

The doctor is right. Bucket lists are stupid. I've got bigger fish to fry. I have to plan for my future.

At the top of the fresh 3x5 card I write one word: HEAVEN. Right underneath HEAVEN, I write: THINGS THAT WON'T BE THERE in neat block letters.

The first thing that comes to mind is that there is a very strong chance Heaven will not have sweet hidden stashes of dark chocolate ready for me to discover and enjoy.

I'm beginning to worry there will be nothing to take the edge off of eternity. I make a note: *Buy and eat some really fine dark chocolate.*

SIX

Lots of it.

Champagne is probably also out of the question. It's not one of those vows of poverty/sackcloth and ashes kind of drinks. At best, I can probably expect an occasional cup of weak tea. Then again, I've drunk so little good Champagne in my life, certainly not enough to make it a habit. I'm pretty certain I could survive in Heaven without the bubbly. However, I might actually need a halfway decent glass of Chianti, chilled, at sunset each day, just to keep the momentum of forever after going. I write that down.

As soon as I write down Chianti I get the feeling that it's a little too Italian for eternity and cross it out. Italy is all about busy, loud and always going somewhere fast while standing in traffic.

Once you get to Heaven, you're there. No traffic jams. I'm also beginning to doubt, given the pushy Italian thing, that there will be really good spaghetti and meatballs in eternity.

I make another note: *Go to Assaggio's to eat spaghetti and meatballs and drink a bottle of their best Chianti. Call ahead and have them put it on ice so it will be perfect. Think of spaghetti and meatballs as a kind of end of life prescription: PRN.*

Despite all the talk about pearly gates and St. Peter and all that, no one has ever ventured back from Heaven to give us the real skinny on what to expect. What Heaven has to offer is anyone's guess, or, maybe, everyone's personal fantasy including that thing about dogs going to Heaven. All dogs? I'm having trouble with this idea. If you can have dogs, why not cats? Rabbits? Pet snakes? Turtles?

While I'm trying to imagine the Heaven I'm headed for, dogs or no dogs, I'm beginning to think the angels who are looking down on the rest of us rarely worry about lack of sleep or the need for a little caffeine boost in the middle of the afternoon.

In short, I'm almost positive there won't be lattes or even black coffee in Heaven.

I get up to order another drink. This time, a double shot espresso. The blended latte was a good start, but I'm feeling the need for something stronger. The man standing behind me in line taps me on the shoulder.

"Heaven is waiting," he says.

"On it," I reply.

He takes out a religious tract from his backpack. It's one of those cheesy things with a faded, full color picture of Jesus, arms spread, rays of sunshine radiating from his head. I'm not impressed.

"We will all be brothers and sisters together in Heaven," he says.

He pushes the tract into my hands. I grab the brochure and pull back from him as quickly as possible, trying to avoid having to touch.

"No sex?" I ask.

"The sins of the flesh will disappear. Our earthly bodies will be gone. We will not want for anything," he says, spreading his arms in a weak imitation of the printed Jesus he has just handed me.

"I'm not liking the sound of that," I say as I inch my way away from the Jesus man and up to the counter to place my order.

"Shall we pray," he says, reaching out to touch my shoulders.

"No thanks," I say, turning away from him. "Give me a double shot of espresso," I tell the barista.

"Anything else?"

"Add one of those fat chocolate frosted brownies to my bill and a cup of coffee for the freak standing behind me." I flip the barista my credit card.

"Praise Jesus! Bless you Sister..." he grabs his coffee and salutes me.

I get my drink and brownie and get as far away from the Jesus

SIX

man as possible. I have work to do.

I add the word SEX to my to do list then cross it out. Who's going to have sex with me on such short notice? Certainly not the Jesus man.

I turn the 3x5 card over and start a new list.

FORGIVENESS.

Underneath I begin to make a list of the people I need to forgive and the ones from whom I need to ask forgiveness.

I start from childhood and work my way up to last week. The list is impressive. Depressing. I sip my double espresso. I'm really going to miss espressos and lattes. Everyone has past sins, but, if you think about it, we all eventually move on.

I begin eliminating people from my list. No need to cause any more trouble for old friends and acquaintances by bringing up the past. I'm feeling pretty good that I bought Jesus-boy that coffee. That must count for something.

In the end, my list is pretty short. Concise.

Forgive the Rabbi's son. Beg forgiveness of my daughter.

It had nothing to do with religion.

It was all about motorcycles, tight pants and my big breasts.

"I saw the Rabbi's son," my mother calls out.

I'm in the bathroom, happy for the moment that I don't have a zit. I'm sixteen. Sixteen and my boobs are growing. Bongers. They're big and firm. Jimmy loves them. I love the way he cups them in his rough hands and cradles them like they're new born kittens. They are bigger than I ever dreamed they'd be. They're glorious.

"We're not Jewish," I yell at the door.

"You don't have to be Jewish to talk to the Rabbi's son."

"You only have to be desperate," I say.

"I told him you've been looking for someone to play tennis with...

that you were thinking of taking some tennis lessons. He's captain of the team you know."

"You did not!" I scream, pushing the door open with the force of an atomic bomb explosion.

"He's coming at four," she says. "I paid for three lessons. Thought that would be enough time to get you focused on your serve, get you..."

"Away from Jimmy?"

"I didn't say that," she says.

"You think the Rabbi's son is a better person than Jimmy. Don't you?"

"I didn't say that."

"Why, oh why would you think, just because his father is a rabbi, that Eli isn't like the other boys and doesn't want to get into my pants?"

"Jimmy's got some growing up to do."

"You mean he needs to own a car rather than a motorcycle? Oh, no, that's not what you either think or mean. You're thinking that if he had a car we would be doing it in the backseat. You should be happy I'm going out with a boy who has a motorcycle."

"It has nothing to do with the motorcycle."

"Really? Could it be that you're not worried about Jimmy and the motorcycle, but instead, you're worried about my beautiful breasts... the very same ones that boys can't keep their eyes or their hands off of and that maybe, just maybe, if I take tennis lessons from the Rabbi's son, that somehow my boobs will melt away and all your twisted troubles will vanish."

"You could use some exercise."

"You could use a shrink..." I scream back as I push past her to my bedroom and slam the door.

SIX

"Four o'clock," she yells through the door. "Wear something, anything other than those jeans you've got on. You can't play tennis in tight pants."

"You call that a serve?" Eli yells at me across the court.

I look at my watch hoping the hour is up. Nope. Fifteen minutes have gone by. Only fifteen. I have forty-five more minutes of his abuse to endure.

Eli walks around the net. He stands behind me and starts to lift my arm to show me how to properly raise my racquet in order to execute the serve. His sweaty hand slides down my arm to my chest. He squeezes my right breast. Hard.

"How 'bout I pay you to give me lessons?" he says, breathing down my neck. I can smell his bagel breath.

"Don't know what you're talking about," I say, trying to wiggle away from his grasp. He puts his other arm around my waist and pulls me towards him. I swing my racquet at his head.

He lets go of my breast and grabs the racquet out of my hand. He begins pushing me off the court, pushing, pushing, over the edge of the hill towards the river. I try to fight back. He pushes me again, hard this time. It scares me and I fall. He falls on top of me. We tumble down to the riverbed.

How ironic, I think, as he easily pulls my pants down around my ankles, the sweat pants my mother made me wear, not my tight jeans that Eli would have never been able to pull down, that I'm going to do it for the first time not in the back of a car, but on a bed, a riverbed.

I close my eyes and listen to the water tumbling over the rocks. I grab a handful of mud. I think about fighting. I think about Jimmy. I think about anything except Eli raping me.

He doesn't even bother to kiss me. He just does it, then rolls off, satisfied that he's had me. I start to cry. He slaps my face.

"If you tell anyone," he says, "I'll say I never touched you. No one would believe you anyway. I'm the rabbi's son. I'm the nice boy. You're the girl with the big tits. Who would believe you? Everyone knows you're crazy."

I'm not crazy.

I should have never listened to my mother and changed out of my tight jeans.

I tell. I shout it from the mountaintop. I write it on the bathroom stall door at school. When I find out I'm pregnant, I call his parents. I tell them everything.

I call his tennis coach. No one believes me. Everyone is so sure Jimmy did this to me that his parents take his motorcycle away and send him to military school. I quit speaking. I stay in my room. I make lists. I beg my mother and father to send me away to have the baby. But, they make me stay. They wake me up every morning, scream at me until I get dressed and take me to school so everyone can see what I have done. It is their way of making me pay for my sins.

When my baby girl is born, dark curly hair framing her small face, I sneak out of my hospital room and take a picture of her in the nursery. I send it to Eli's parents. It's his, I say. It's not Jimmy's child. Jimmy would never rape me.

But, it isn't his and she isn't mine. My parents made sure of that. Three days after she was born (she, my daughter, baby girl she, she who came from me, she who shamed me) the social worker came to the hospital and took her away and gave her to a family.

I have these dreams. They never stop. I take my baby girl down to the riverbed where she came from. I put her in the water like they did in the Bible with baby Moses in a cradle made of reeds and weeds, and push her away. She floats down the river, bobbing in the water. I can hear my baby crying. In my dream I do not know where the water has taken her or who has plucked her out of the river and loved her.

But, I do know. I've always known.

It wasn't hard to figure out who took her. And, it made it hard for me ever to leave and follow my dream to a better place. So I stayed.

It was painful at first, knowing that I would always be that high school girl who got pregnant. That I would never have the chance to grow up to be anyone else and would never have a life bigger than the town I grew up in. But later, my staying just became a way of living by myself. It was easy enough.

None of my friends called me or came to visit after she was born. Boys no longer looked at my breasts, smiled at me or asked me out. Instead, they bumped against me in the hallways and laughed. I learned to turn my head and keep walking. Fast.

People talk.

The Hapworths owned the best bakery in town. Mr. and Mrs. Hapworth baked and sold dark brown pumpernickel bread, salted rye rolls and beautiful sweet cream birthday cakes. Mr. Hapworth made the bread and Mrs. Hapworth the cakes.

Mrs. Hapworth did not make sheet cakes. Sheet cakes were something housewives made from box mixes to take to church suppers. Mrs. Hapworth made elegant double layer cakes from scratch and filled the layers in between with either her homemade raspberry jam or lemon curd. Once the layers were assembled and the sides smoothly frosted with her long metal spatula, Mrs. Hapworth would hold the cake like a wheel and roll it in crushed walnuts. Once the nuts were in place, she'd settle the cake onto a circle of cardboard covered in a lacy paper doily and frost the top layer. Afterwards, she'd pipe flowers all around the edges, both top and bottom: daisies in springtime, pink and yellow roses for summer, golden mums in the fall and brilliant red poinsettias at Christmas time. When you ordered a cake for your birthday, she'd write Happy Birthday and your name across the top in shiny red glycerin.

When you had the occasion to go to Hapworth's to buy a loaf of bread, you always hoped that Mrs. Hapworth would be there at the low counter in the front of the bakery: moving carefully from flower to flower making her magic. Her cakes were not cakes, but works of art. It was wonderful to watch.

Whenever Mrs. Hapworth came to the moment where she piped someone's name across the top of one of her cakes, she always closed her eyes before she started, as though she was not just writing someone's name, but making a wish for them as well.

One afternoon, shortly after my baby was born I happened to walk by Hapworth's Bakery and saw that there was a cradle next to the place where Mrs. Hapworth worked on her cakes. Inside the cradle was a beautiful baby girl with dark curly hair like Eli's, and honey brown eyes just like mine.

Seeing her there felt like someone had walked across my grave. It stirred something deep inside of me.

I should have told the doctor that death doesn't scare me. I've lived with ghosts nearly all my life. Ghosts, shadows, doubts. They're all the same. Since the day I had her, I have carried the ghost shadow of my daughter in my heart as though keeping her there was a penance I was required to do in order to keep her safe.

Having her changed me. Made me quieter than I had been before. Made me want to do things and make things right for her sake.

SIX

Because of her, I forgave my parents. They, however, never forgave me. Their shame was too great.

I kept walking by the bakery every day after that first time I saw my little girl. Walked as fast as I could all the way home and ran to my room and shut the door. Sometimes, I stopped just long enough to press my face against the big picture window pretending to watch Mrs. Hapworth decorate her cakes, hoping to see my daughter.

One day, my mother sent me to the bakery to buy bread. When I walked into the store, Mrs. Hapworth stopped what she was doing. No one else was there.

"Would you like to hold her?" she asked.

Hold her? Touch her? I had not been allowed to hold my baby in the hospital. I was not allowed to even touch her before they took her away.

"She has your eyes," Mrs. Hapworth whispered, twisting her long metal spatula into her big mixing bowl then holding out a bit of frosting to me as if she was making an offering of friendship.

I let my finger swipe the frosting from the knife and bring it to my lips. Sweet kisses. Baby kisses. Sweet wet baby kisses.

"It's okay," she said. "I won't tell anyone."

"What's her name?" I asked.

"Juliana," she said, wiping her hands on her apron. "Like the beautiful strong Queen of the Netherlands."

I did not have the heart to tell her Juliana was conceived on a riverbank, hardly a royal beginning.

"Go ahead," she said, "It's okay. I know everything. I am not afraid for you to touch her."

Juliana was heavier than I imagined she would be. I cupped my hand behind her small head, put my other hand and arm around her body and lifted her up out of her cradle to my shoulder. Her cheek brushed against my cheek.

"She won't be small for long," Mrs. Hapworth said. "I think you should come by as often as possible and hold her. Just for a moment. Let her know she is loved. She is loved, you know."

"I know," I say.

"When she is older, she will ask too many questions. But for now, all she knows is what it feels like to be held. When she is older..." Mrs. Hapworth started to say.

"I understand," I interrupt, "you don't have to worry. I will never tell her."

"Will you promise me?"

"I promise," I say.

"Then it is all good. You may come, everyday if you like, and hold her, but only if there are no customers. I don't want people to talk. Three o'clock is a good time, a quiet time in the shop. Look first before you come in."

"I promise," I tell her again then put Juliana back in her cradle and leave the store without ever buying the bread.

When I graduate from high school, my parents tell me they are not willing to pay for college because they can't trust me. They won't throw good money away on someone like me.

I run to my room and close my door. What about my list? My good grades? My dreams? Dreams are never enough. Are they?

I stay at home and commute to the local teacher's college. I get a small scholarship to cover my tuition. I work at the campus coffee shop to pay for my books and gas. I don't go to parties or have friends. But I have everything I need. I have my classes. I have my books. I have my bedroom. And I keep my door shut.

After Juliana was born, all of the doors in our house remained

SIX

shut. My shame had become my parent's shame. We didn't have much to say to each other. Once, when my mother dared to open my bedroom door to talk to me, she discovered I hadn't made my bed that day and started screaming: "You've ruined everything in my life. Everything."

Juliana was walking by the time I started college. When I drove by the bakery on my way home from school I'd see her standing by the big front window playing with her tiny pots and pans, pretending to bake cakes and frost them just like Mrs. Hapworth.

I had made a new plan by then. I had a promise to keep. I couldn't hold Juliana anymore, but I had to see her. Going by the bakery to buy bread everyday was not part of the bargain I'd struck with Mrs. Hapworth.

My new plan was to go to school, make good grades, and become a teacher. I told Mrs. Hapworth I wanted to be Juliana's teacher so I could watch over her as she went through school. Mrs. Hapworth gave me her blessing and reminded me again, I had to keep my promise and never tell her.

I finished my degree just as Juliana was starting school. Juliana was shy and a bit self-conscious. She was tall like Eli, almost the tallest one in her class. Her hair was not soft and blond like the popular girls, but rather dark and tangled with curls. The kids made fun of her hair, which made her even more quiet and withdrawn.

When she was in my third grade class, I bought a small green turtle and put it in an aquarium on my desk. The students named the turtle Herbert and took turns feeding him. When Christmas came, all the students put their names in a hat hoping to be chosen to be the one to take him home over the vacation. Juliana squealed with delight when I pulled the winning slip of paper and called out her name.

It was hard not to want to hug her.

So many lists. So many scribbled 3x5 cards. So many dreams.

At the end of every third grade year I gave each child in my class a 3x5 card and asked them to make a list of their dreams and desires. I told them it could be a list of things they wanted to do for the summer, for fourth grade, or for wherever their dreams might take them.

On our last day of school together every year, I threw a party. Parents were not invited. I baked cupcakes the night before and together we decorated the cupcakes with everything edible imaginable: colored sugar, gumdrops, gummy bears, pretzel sticks, blueberries, raisins, peanuts and licorice whips. After lunch we would push our chairs into a tight circle in the middle of the room and we'd eat our cupcakes, drink lemonade and dream together.

One by one, the students would stand in the middle of the circle and read from their 3x5 card. No matter what was on their list or what they dreamed of, we'd applaud and ask how they were going to get where they wanted to go. We'd listen as though all of our lives depended on knowing how to get there too.

No dream or list was ever too small or too big. There would be dreams of staying up late every night in the summer in order to catch fireflies and count every star in the sky. Dreams of becoming an astronaut and wanting more than anything to walk on the Moon or be the first to go to Mars. Girls who dreamed of becoming beautiful ballerinas and those who just wanted to be rich enough to eat a different flavor of ice cream every day for a year.

I loved each and every one of their dreams and told them so, pressing a bright gold star onto the corner of their 3x5 card once they read their dream aloud.

Every once in awhile there'd be a dream that was so small it would

SIX

make my heart ache and I would have to turn away for a moment while the children applauded.

Those small dreams always came selfless and whispered as if the dreamers had held their secret dream in their hands for such a long time, rolling it from side to side until it was smooth and wanting and hard to even talk about.

When Juliana was in my third grade, she was the last to stand in the circle to dream. No one giggled or said anything about her hair. The room was hushed, waiting to hear the last dream, the one that would signal that school was over and summer about to begin.

"I want," she said, drawing in a long slow breath, "to grow up to be just like my mother."

"Then you could bake us all birthday cakes!" the students shouted almost in unison as they clapped and laughed and scooted their chairs back to their desks so they could be dismissed.

"My real mother," Juliana whispered.

When she stepped close to my chair, so I could press a gold star onto the corner of her card, she looked at me as if she knew.

I had long given up the notion that I was Juliana's mother. Instead, I had begun to cast myself as a kind of guardian angel assigned to protect her. Once, when Toby Wilson snatched a handful of Juliana's curly hair and pulled as hard as he could, bringing tears to her eyes, it was all I could do to not summon my sword of righteousness and chop off his head.

Instead, I called out his name and told him to let go of Juliana's hair immediately before I dragged him to the principal's office and called his mother. He let go, turned on his sassy heel and marched himself off to his next class without looking back. Embarrassed, Juliana ran to the bathroom crying.

I did not run after her.

When the next fall came, I was back in my third grade classroom while Juliana moved on to fourth grade down the other hallway. The next year, she moved on to fifth grade, and again, I stayed in my third grade classroom. When she went to middle school, I no longer saw her.

Things happen. Dreams change. I knew I could not follow her. She was not mine to love. I was not hers to know. Occasionally, when I went into the bakery to buy bread or order a cake for a friend's birthday, I would see Juliana. She was pretty in an extravagant way that scared most high school boys but drew the attention of older men. Her hair was an unruly mass of dark seductive curls and her eyes were honey golden brown and serious. Hidden behind her stiff white bakery apron, I could see that her breasts were large and firm like mine had once been.

Whenever I came into the store, Mrs. Hapworth would rush to wait on me, as though she had become afraid of letting me near Juliana ever again. I never spoke to Juliana when I came to the store and she never spoke to me, but I could feel her watching me as I paid for my bread or cake and carried my purchase out the door.

One day, I ran into Juliana at the grocery store.

"Do you remember what I wished for on party day in third grade?" she asked.

I hesitated.

"Do you?" she asked again.

"That was so many third grades ago," I said, laughing, hoping to brush away her question.

"I think you do," she said.

Did she know?

SIX

"She ran away," Mrs. Hapworth said, her long frosting blade slashing across the top of a cake, cutting it in half. "Why didn't you run away? Why? Why did you have to stay? Why?"

"Juliana was here," I said. "I couldn't dream of going away."

I knock on Eli's door. He never left either. His three children were students of mine when they were in third grade.

"I forgive you," I say.

His hair is no longer black, but a dirty looking steel grey. His eyes are still hard with an edge of meanness in them.

"I guess we ruined each other's lives," he says, stepping onto the porch, closing the door behind him.

"You didn't ruin mine," I say.

"What about Juliana?" he asks.

"You knew?"

"She came to the house once. It was late. She was drunk. I guess it was the night she ran away. She rang the doorbell over and over again until I woke up and opened the door."

"What did she want?"

"She asked if I was her father and if you were her mother."

"What did you tell her?"

"I lied."

"Why?"

"I didn't want my kids to know."

Eli didn't know where Juliana had gone and neither did Mrs. Hapworth. No one knew. Juliana never called. She never wrote. She never said goodbye.

Six weeks. Six months. I have decided not to do anything, so I only have six. It's not enough time to find Juliana, to beg her forgiveness and make things right.

But, there's never enough time, is there?

THE JUNGFRAU

Her mother tapped the band of her heavy gold ring against the edge of the table. When that failed to get her daughter's attention, she cleared her throat and pointed to the thick grey haze covering the mountains outside the dining room window.

"Rain, probably even snow on the Jungfrau again today," she said in a loud voice as though her daughter might be hard of hearing, even though she wasn't.

Lydia looked up without acknowledging her mother and went back to buttering her croissant. A waiter walked towards their table carrying a pot of fresh hot coffee and a pot of steamed milk.

The older woman ignored the waiter and continued talking as though she and her daughter were engaged in a pleasant conversation.

"This will be my last chance to see the Jungfrau. We leave for home day after tomorrow, and tomorrow we're scheduled to go to Gruyere. I'll probably never be able to make a trip like this again."

Her daughter didn't respond.

The older woman sighed heavily, looked straight at her daughter, then leaned closer to her over the table. "I'm not well, you know, and certainly not young enough to even dream of coming here again."

Once again, her daughter said nothing; instead, she motioned to the waiter that she wanted more coffee.

Her mother continued, "It's a shame the weather has been so bad. Your Uncle George was right. I tried to tell you before you made these arrangements that you just can't count on the weather in the mountains in spring."

"This is June," Lydia said, looking up from her croissant at the cold frosted mountaintop. She hadn't been listening, couldn't bear to hear the same conversation once again. The weather had been cloudy. There had been some good days too, but none good enough or clear enough to go to the top of the Jungfrau.

"I know it's June. That's obvious."

She hated for anyone to correct her, especially her daughter.

"But," she continued coolly, "it's early June, and June is still spring in the mountains."

Her mother wiped the edge of her mouth with the smooth linen napkin and placed it on her lap, signaling that she was finished with this particular conversation.

"I don't want to go shopping today," she continued, starting a new conversation. "I've really had enough of it. How about you?"

"Fine," said Lydia, looking out the window to the rain dampened street below. "Let's go sight seeing. Maybe go to Spiez, take a ride on the boat that goes across the Thunersee to Oberhofen and see the castle there. It's supposed to be rather charming."

"I don't see the point in taking the boat from Spiez to Oberhofen. If it's overcast here, then it's overcast there. We wouldn't be able to see a thing. If you want to see a castle, let's drive there. Taking a boat ride just to be taking it when there's nothing to see doesn't suit me."

"We don't have to see anything. We could just enjoy taking a boat ride."

Lydia picked up her knife and cut the end off a stiff dark pumpernickel roll, buttered it, and covered it with orange marmalade.

THE JUNGFRAU

"Really, Lydia! You shouldn't eat so much butter. You know it's not good for you. You're not young anymore. You should pay more attention to what you eat."

"Do you want to go to Spiez and take a boat ride?" Lydia asked as she looked at her mother and took a big bite out of the thickly buttered end of her roll.

"I still don't know why you insisted on coming here this soon in the season. I don't know what was so important that you had to come now and couldn't come later. It's a shame. I'll never see this mountain again."

"I have a job. Or have you forgotten?" Lydia didn't mean to say this, not really. Sarcasm rarely worked. It was not the right tactic to use when she wanted to try to get close to her mother.

Her mother began drumming her ring against the edge of the table again.

"Of course I know you have a job. But, this was important to me. I don't understand why you couldn't have tried harder to schedule your vacation later. I would have thought you would have been more considerate of me."

"Why not go up the Jungfrau today?" Lydia suggested. She wanted badly to move the conversation up the mountain, away from the table. "The weather is so unpredictable here, one minute there's rain, then the next it's as clear as a bell. It takes almost two and a half hours by the cog train to get up the Jungfrau. Maybe by the time we get to the top, it will be clear. And, even if it's not, you can say that you went. That you saw the great mountain and that the weather was wretched."

"There's no point in going if you can't see anything. I don't want to go if I can't see anything."

"Then," countered Lydia, in a practiced bait and switch move, "let's go over to Spiez and take the boat to Oberhofen and see the castle, or just explore the old city. It's supposed to be quite beautiful. You've told me so yourself."

"I said that when your father and I were here, Spiez was lovely. But that was years ago. Since then, I've heard that it has become built up, a little commercial. Your Aunt Margie's neighbor was here two years ago, and she told Margie that it wasn't as nice as it used to be."

"Maybe she was wrong."

"Why would she tell Margie something that wasn't true?" her mother once again began tapping her heavy gold ring against the edge of the table.

"I didn't accuse her of lying. I merely suggested she might be wrong and that we should check out Spiez for ourselves, not depend on Aunt Margie's neighbor to do it for us."

The old woman looked hard at her daughter as though she was trying to see through her, to detect if there was some lie lurking behind her eyes. She couldn't understand her daughter: didn't know why she was so independent, why she wasn't more considerate, more accepting of her.

"Well," she said at last, her voice as flat as the dark wet street outside, "if it's that important to you, then we should go to Spiez. But, I don't see the point of taking a boat ride if it's not even going to be clear enough to see across the lake."

The two women drove the short ride to the boat dock in silence. Lydia cruised at a pace that was just slightly faster than her mother approved of. It was a foolish thing to do, almost childish. But, there were times when Lydia went out of her way to get a rise out of her mother. Lydia often wondered what would happen if she pushed her mother just a little bit farther…perhaps just far enough to create a small crack in the

THE JUNGFRAU

wall they had built together over the lifetime they had shared.

"Look at the mountains," Lydia said, "and the lovely village." Along the shore of the brilliant blue Thunersee were dozens of clean white washed homes with curved weathered red tiled roofs. Every house had a garden bursting with blazing red geraniums.

"Mountains!" her mother snorted. "Those aren't mountains. Those are foothills, and low ones at that. We haven't yet seen the mountains. Hasn't cleared the whole time we've been here. Been a bad spring. Even the woman at the desk said so. I told you that spring just isn't reliable here."

"Maybe it will clear tomorrow," Lydia offered. She lifted her foot from the accelerator, slowing the car a little. She was sorry she had been speeding just to aggravate her mother. Sorry they had to come when the weather was so unpredictable. Sorry they could never seem to enjoy being together.

"Tomorrow doesn't matter," her mother reminded her, "we're scheduled for the tour to Gruyere. So, even if it does clear, we can't go up the Jungfrau."

"We can cancel," Lydia offered. She wanted more than anything to try once again to break down the wall between them and perhaps make her mother happy.

"Then we'll lose our deposit. The brochure said that you have to give a 48 hour notice to cancel your reservations or you lose your deposit."

So what, Lydia wanted to scream. So what! She started to point out to her mother that the deposit was eight American dollars. No big deal. She started to, but she didn't bother. She didn't want to get into it with her mother anymore. She wanted peace with her. More than anything, right now, she wished they were sitting in a café at the water's edge in Oberhofen drinking espresso, laughing and talking together while they watched the boats pull to shore, load up, then pull away and sail across the crystal clear sea.

"We're here," Lydia said, forcing a smile into her voice as she eased the car into the parking lot to the entrance of the boat dock and the old city of Spiez.

Her mother opened her car door and swung her legs out. When she stood up, she stretched slightly, arching her back, and placed her cane in her left hand. Then, clicking her ring against its ebony handle, she stepped away from the car.

"When your father and I were here," she said, her voice sounding light and young as she walked awkwardly to the side of the car where Lydia stood, "we spent a whole day just walking through the streets of the old city. We didn't do a thing, just walked. The flowers were beautiful that day. Spiez is a city of exceptional gardens, of brilliant flowers and lush green trees. It was really brilliant that day. The air was clear and warm. Everything was perfect."

"Why don't we take a walk?" Lydia asked, jumping at the chance to keep the moment light. "We can see the gardens and you can show me the places you and Dad explored."

"No," her mother said, waving her hand in the air as though she were shooing flies. "I'm too old to walk that far anymore. Besides, it wouldn't be the same. Those are the kinds of things you do when you have someone special to share them with."

"You have me," Lydia said.

"Yes," her mother replied, smiling a moment at her daughter before taking her cane in her right hand and steadily walking away from her. "I do have you. But, that's not what I'm talking about. Perhaps if you and David had managed to stay together and he were here with us today, we'd walk through the town."

She looked back at Lydia who was locking the car.

THE JUNGFRAU

"I said," her mother went on, "you should be with someone special when you have something special to share."

Lydia put her hand on the roof of the car in order to steady herself. She felt as though she had been hit and had momentarily lost her balance from the blow. She closed her eyes against the bright noon sun. If David were here, if things had worked out: if they had stayed together.

Her mother had never asked her why they split up. She never once wanted to know why it happened or how Lydia felt about it.

It struck Lydia, as she drew in a deep breath in order to regain her balance before she had to run to catch up to her mother, that her mother had never once in her life asked her how she felt about anything.

By the time she caught up, her mother was sitting on a straight-backed wooden bench, waiting for Lydia to purchase their boat tickets.

"First class," her mother shouted above the rumble of the approaching boat and the chatter of the people who were standing around waiting for the boat to dock.

"You know I only like to travel first class on things like boats or trains. Don't care that much for the local color."

Lydia wondered how many people standing around waiting to catch a ride across the Thunersee spoke English, how many people her mother had just offended.

"Two, first class," Lydia told the agent in her clear but limited German.

When the boat docked, she showed the tickets to the boat captain, and they were ushered unceremoniously up a set of tight steep stairs to the upper deck.

"I told you first class," her mother snapped. "If you didn't have enough money, you should have told me so. I would have gladly given it to you."

"This is first class," Lydia said, helping her mother into the small-upholstered wooden deck chair near the railing along the top deck.

"You know I have trouble with stairs," her mother said. "Especially narrow ones on rocking boats."

"I didn't know there would be stairs."

Lydia's first reaction was to blame herself for not asking about the stairs, then on second thought, she realized that there was no way in the world she could have known or even suspected that first class would be up a flight of stairs. There was no reason to think there would be a problem, no reason to blame herself for her mother's short fuse or her foul moods.

"I had no idea that first class was on the top deck," Lydia said at last, speaking slowly, counting to ten silently to herself as each word crept out. She wanted for once not to be apologizing for something she didn't do.

"Well," her mother said, rapping her cane loudly on the deck, "I certainly hope we don't have to ride up here on the return."

"I imagine," Lydia answered, catching the rage in her voice before it could escape, "that since we have first class seats, we can sit anywhere we damn well please."

"There's no need to curse, young lady. I was just saying that I hoped we didn't have to ride back on this deck in these same seats. You have a tendency to overreact to everything I say. You should work on that a little. It would improve your social graces immensely."

By the time the boat pulled away from the dock, the sky had cleared. All along the banks of the Thunersee, Lydia could see the clean clusters of houses with their delicate terraced gardens. All over the mountainside, geraniums mingled with ageratum and the cool frosted gray of her favorite: Lamb's Ear. The mountainside was

THE JUNGFRAU

carpeted in color.

The view from the boat was magnificent. All around them were mountains. Not great ones like the Jungrau, but majestic ones like the graceful Saxeten, the blunt nosed Harder and the towering Morgenberghorn. Lydia felt safe, cradled almost, in the arms of the ancient mountains.

The air was fresh and spring-like, the breeze warm, yet refreshing, and for the first time in ten days, the sun was shining in a deep blue sky.

They rode to the castle in Oberhofen in silence. It was, just as the brochure had said, a perfectly lovely castle, appointed with an exquisite collection of antiques, paintings and fine furniture.

It was a lovely place to just wander about. There were, of course, stairs: some broad and polished and made from curving oak, some roughly hewn pine that were narrow, straight and steep. Her mother walked up one flight, then, leaning heavily on her cane, she asked Lydia to help her back down. There was nothing in the castle, she declared, that was worth seeing.

Lydia walked with her mother to the garden, fully intending to leave her mother sitting on a bench to watch the boats traverse the Thunersee while she continued to tour the castle on her own. But her mother, upon sitting, smiled up at her and said with the slightest of sighs: "There's nothing more lonely than someone else's garden, is there?"

Lydia sat down beside her. Once her mother had rested, they walked among the flowers and the sculptures in the garden, to the castle gates and the small gift shop. Lydia went inside and bought a book with color pictures detailing the restored castle interior, including the sparse, almost pristine chapel and the seductive, slightly garish, private harem room in the uppermost turret of the fortress.

Her mother refused to go into the gift shop, declaring once again, that she was tired of shopping.

Afterwards, they walked down the cobblestone path from the castle to the edge of the lakeshore, her mother holding on to Lydia's arm for balance, careful not to clutch her too tightly, or touch more than the sleeve of her daughter's coat.

Walking side-by-side down the slick path of worn cobblestones, Lydia had the urge to put an arm around her mother, in order to keep her from slipping as she walked over the rough stones. They had never been the kind of family that touched, only brushed cheeks occasionally in a rather ceremonial greeting that seemed to be required, but only partially observed.

Lydia moved closer to her mother in order to give her more support, but as she did, her mother transferred her cane from her left hand to her right, and as the cane dangled from her tightly closed fist, it hit against the leg of Lydia's pants, managing to create a greater distance between them while they walked.

"There's a café near the boat dock," Lydia said. "Why don't we have lunch there?"

Lydia moved closer to her mother and linked her arm with hers as an offer of support.

"I hate tourist traps," her mother said, slowing her walk in order to shake her arm free from her daughter.

"It's not necessarily a tourist trap."

"If it's near anything that has anything like a view, then it's a tourist trap."

Her mother poked and jabbed her cane at the old cobblestones while tapping her ring against the wood with each step. Her mother's short labored steps syncopated against the sharp thump of her cane and tap of her ring made a strange rhythm: an awkward walking song.

Lydia kept moving toward the café as though she had no intention of eating anywhere else.

"It looks like a fine café. There are even tables and chairs outside. I'd like to just sit here for a while and have some lunch and watch the boats sail across the lake. It's turned out to be such a beautiful day," Lydia said, taking her mother's elbow firmly in hand, while continuing to guide her down the road to the café.

"I don't see the point of paying a fortune for a second rate tourist trap of a meal just so you can watch the boats."

"Lunch," Lydia said with a smile, "is on me."

They sat in the café watching the boats for nearly two hours. The pork loin was slightly overdone and the potatoes a little too buttery, but the beer Lydia drank was cold and bitter and she enjoyed it so much that she ordered another.

After Lydia paid for their meal, they left the café and boarded the return boat. They did not climb the stairs up to first class, but sat instead, on one of the long backless wooden benches on the lower deck.

It was nearly four-thirty when the boat pulled out of the harbor. The sun was still bright and warm but was lost in the shadow of the upper deck, and the exhaust from the heavy lumbering boat engines curled up from the ruffled blue Thunersee and stayed trapped between the two floors.

Her mother complained loudly about the exhaust and that the boat was over crowded with mothers and children, businessmen, shop girls and packages, but Lydia ignored her.

Lydia had wanted this trip with her mother to be pleasant. Her mother was getting older. She was going to die someday. Not soon, perhaps, but sometime in the not too distant future.

Lydia hated her mother for that. Hated the box that had arrived unannounced six months ago at her apartment, packed by professional movers, containing her grandmother's good gold-banded china.

The package was accompanied by one of her mother's cryptic notes: *By rights these are yours. I want things settled before I'm dead.*

Nothing, Lydia realized, as the boat cut its way past the sun-dappled Saxeten and the richly wooded Morgenberghorn, would ever be settled between them.

When they got back to the hotel, the clerk at the desk told them it was going to be clear and warm tomorrow: a perfect day for the Jungfrau. They would go, however, her mother insisted, to Gruyere, as planned.

They would return home to the States the following day and Lydia knew her mother would tell all her friends that their trip was lovely, but the weather a bit uncertain. She would, also, of course, always mention that they never did go up the Jungfrau.

Once home, Lydia would try to forget there were ever any harsh words between them, or any difficult moments. Instead, she would remember only how bright the sun was, and how sweet the breeze felt as it blew against her face on the ride from Spiez to Oberhofen the day they took the boat ride on the Thunersee.

THE BLACK BACKPACK

Margaret tried to tell her husband about what had happened today when she went to the grocery, but he was heading out to the office and didn't have time.

Margaret blocked his exit from their apartment and insisted he listen because it had felt like something dangerous and it worried her.

"Were they Arab?" he asked as he was putting on his coat. "Muslim?"

"Is something going on?" she asked.

"Were they?" he asked again.

Margaret hesitated. She didn't like being afraid. John's recent assignment to come to Brussels to work at the EU had happened so suddenly it had taken her by surprise. She had just begun to know her way around Geneva and hadn't expected to move again so quickly. They were always moving somewhere for his work, whatever it was that he did. It was all so secretive and hush-hush. Of all the places they had been in the last couple of years, she had liked Switzerland. It was clean, tidy. Predictable. It felt safe. She could imagine herself living there. It felt like a place where she could make friends. She hadn't really wanted to come to Brussels.

"You'd tell me if you knew something, wouldn't you?" she asked.

"Margaret..." John said, pulling on his gloves, getting ready to go.

"I know you can't say anything. But, who would I tell?"

She didn't know anyone yet in Brussels. But then, she rarely had time to make friends before he was reassigned and they were moved once again. She was always a stranger. Everyone around her was a stranger. She shopped. Kept to herself and kept busy. Right now, she was learning how to knit. Socks. She had thought socks would be easy, or at least fast, because they were small. But it wasn't at all as simple as knitting a scarf. She had to count stitches. Pay attention. Keep track of the pattern.

At least in Geneva there had been a few shopkeepers who spoke English. Her French was awful. No one in Brussels seemed to understand what she was trying to say, so she often gave up trying and simply pointed politely if she wanted something.

"Were they Muslim?" John asked again.

"This is a Muslim neighborhood. There's no place to buy pork. Which is why I go to the big Carrefour grocery store by the park. I can pick out what I want without having to talk to anyone. I saw them when I approached the store. There were three of them at first. They were walking in front of me and then another man came running up to join them. When the guy who had been running caught up to the three men, one of them handed him a folded piece of paper. I was looking at the piece of paper when he turned and saw me. I tried to make eye contact. You always tell me that the best thing I can do to be safe is make eye contact, so I did. He knew I had seen them give him something. He started yelling at me in Arabic. Then he ran away."

"What did they look like?"

"They had dark skin and hair. I don't know. They gave him that piece of paper and then he yelled at me and ran."

"What did you do?"

"I went into the grocery store and bought two pork chops."

THE BLACK BACKPACK

Later that evening, Margaret heard John's phone ring just as she was carrying a tray with their cake and coffee into the living room. John looked at her without speaking then walked over to the stereo in order to fiddle with the dials until he found the news. There had been an attack in Paris. People were dead. There had been gunfire and suicide bombings. Chaos. Fear.

Margaret carried the tray back into the kitchen and went into the hallway to get John's coat and scarf. It was late. She was sure it was cold outside. She grabbed his gloves off the hall table.

"Stay inside," he said, slipping his arms into the sleeves of his coat. "I'll keep my phone on in case you need to reach me. I'll call if there's anything I can tell you."

"Those men," Margaret said. "When I went to the store yesterday."

"I'm sure it was nothing."

"You can't let the attack that happened yesterday in Paris scare you. That's what they want," John said to her the next morning, as he got ready for work.

He looked exhausted. Like he'd hardly slept. She wasn't sure what time he had come home. She'd fallen asleep watching the news on the small television in their bedroom. Not that she could understand what was being said. The world shifted and wobbled in the flicker of the newscast. She fell asleep thinking that there was something she should have done. Maybe told the police about the men she saw, the note that was passed. She worried that John would not know how to fix what had happened this time. No one would.

Margaret tired of being at home alone all day, so she often cajoled

John into taking a leisurely stroll with her after he got home from work before going out to dinner. Once they had walked and she had talked, John would find a little hole in the wall place and take pleasure in ordering just the right wine for whatever it was they were eating that night. The ease and intimacy of it all made her feel like they were on a vacation together rather than living in yet another foreign place where Margaret didn't know anyone.

They could have just as easily been in Paris rather than in Brussels last night. Could have been one of the couples sitting in the restaurant when the gunmen opened fire and the suicide bomber detonated his vest.

"I'm not scared," Margaret lied.

"We're sorting things out," John said. It was what he always said when something happened. They had been in places before where things had happened. That's just the way it was. Margaret had come to believe that what John did when he was at work was sort things out.

"I'll be fine," Margaret tried to reassure him.

"Why don't you come to my office this afternoon? Drag me away from my work for a few minutes so we can have lunch together. There's this Chinese place right around the corner from my office I've been dying to try. I've heard they make delicious dumplings. Like nothing else you've ever had."

"Will you be home for dinner?" she asked.

"I don't think so. One o'clock for lunch?"

"I'd like that," Margaret answered.

"Take the tram not the subway. It'll be safer."

Margaret was relieved to have some place to go. There had been too many times and places where they had lived when things got dangerous and all she could do was stay inside and knit or read or whatever it was she was doing in that particular city to keep herself occupied.

Occupied. Like she was her own country and the only place to be was inside her house and inside herself. Safe.

"We can't let them make us prisoners," John had told her more than once. "I want you to get out during the day. Explore on your own. Meet people. Try your best to make eye contact. That way you won't be afraid of them and they won't be afraid of you. That's how it works."

Eye-to-eye. That was her habit. When she passed someone on the street, she didn't look away. Instead she made eye contact, hoping they would look back and, in that brief moment, connect. She was just trying to connect when she saw those men. Saw the folded note pass from hand to hand.

Margaret put on her coat and twisted her wedding rings until the big diamond on her engagement ring fit snugly into the palm of her hand before pulling on her gloves. It was an old habit, something her mother had made her promise she would do whenever she and John were away in yet another foreign country. It had been ten years since her mother had died and many more years since Margaret had lived in a place she thought of as home.

The tram was a short walk from their apartment. It was half past eleven when she arrived, long past the time when most people were rushing to work. The narrow island that served as the tram stop in the middle of the street was now crowded with old men and women dragging shopping carts or pushing strollers. Most of the women wore headscarves. Some wore long wide coats that covered their clothes. The children were all dark eyed and beautiful.

Margaret did her best to look at each of them and smile. Some returned her gaze. Others looked down or turned away. Nothing was said.

Margaret let the mothers and the old ones board the tram first, choosing to get on last out of courtesy. It was, she always understood, their country, their tram. She was the foreign visitor.

When she boarded, there was only one place left on the bench seat along the window on the left hand side that faced the narrow row of seats across the middle aisle. The tram jerked forward. Mothers, babies and shopping carts were tossed about a bit before settling in.

Two stops later, a young man, Arab, perhaps Muslim, boarded and took the recently vacated seat across from Margaret. In a tram filled with women, children and old men, he seemed out of place. He was about the same age as the young man who had taken the note and yelled at her yesterday. She tried to make eye contact, but he was looking out the window.

She closed her eyes for a moment in order to try to recall what the three young men who had handed the note over to the fourth one had looked like. When she opened her eyes and looked closely at the young man sitting across from her, she couldn't be sure if he was or wasn't one of them.

The young man, the old women, the two old men reading their newspapers at the back of the tram, and the mothers with their sleeping babies all traveled in silence. The tram was too full for conversation. It wouldn't have been polite to talk.

The old woman next to Margaret was forced to slide closer to her at the next stop when a young woman with baby in her arms got on and needed a seat. Their legs and shoulders touched.

The young man sitting across from them reached up and pulled the cord to signal he wanted the next stop. The tram pushed through traffic to the corner then came to a halt. The young man got up and walked to

THE BLACK BACKPACK

the closed door at the rear.

Margaret clutched her purse. The young man had left his black backpack on the floor by the aisle. The old woman next to her noticed it too and leaned back as if she were trying to get away from it. The young woman with the baby froze. The old men dropped their papers to their sides and stared. No one spoke.

The tram was stopped. As was the custom on this particular route, the driver waited for the light to change so the traffic would clear and it would be safe for passengers to get off. The doors stayed closed.

No one moved. All eyes were on the backpack and the young man who was standing at the back door waiting to get off.

Margaret turned her head to look at the woman sitting next to her. The woman placed her hand on Margaret's leg. Margaret could feel the woman's strong fingers digging into her thigh, clamping tighter and tighter. The young woman with the baby in her arms brought the baby up to her shoulder, covered its head with her hand and closed her eyes.

Margaret turned her head and tried to make eye contact with the young man who had left the backpack, just as she had tried to make eye contact with the young man who had seen her take the note the other day.

He didn't turn his head to meet her gaze. Margaret turned to the old men with their newspapers, hoping they would say or do something. They too were looking at the backpack. No one moved.

What was the word for backpack?

The only French word Margaret could think of was sac.

"The sac!" Margaret tried to yell. Her heart clutched in her throat. "You've left your backpack," Margaret shouted in English. The young man turned. Margaret pointed to his backpack, hoping he would understand what she was saying. The old woman sitting next to Margaret gripped her leg tighter.

The young man took two steps forward, grabbed the straps of the backpack with his right hand then swung it smoothly over his left shoulder.

"Merci," he said.

The door opened. The young man got off. The old woman next to Margaret let go of Margaret's leg and straightened her coat. The two old men looked at Margaret and nodded, acknowledging what she had done, then picked up their papers again and continued reading. The young woman with the baby opened her eyes and began rocking from side to side, humming as she did.

The tram lurched forward.

LEAVING

"Sorry I'm late," Eleanor called out as soon as her key released the latch on the lock and the door swung open into the long dark hallway piled haphazardly with her husband's books and papers. She didn't know for the life of her why he could never throw anything away.

The minute she saw Daniel face down on the floor of the living room, she wasn't sorry she was late: she hated watching him slip, one drink at a time, into a stupor. She was happy to have missed that part and just as happy not to have to fight with him tonight. She was tired. The television was blaring. He liked the television to be cranked up as loud as it would go. It was a small bone of contention between the two of them and all the more reason why she didn't really care a whit any more if she was late or not.

It wasn't just the television. It was how quickly these days his work shifted into drinking. It didn't seem to matter if she came home at noon or stayed late in her office. Whenever she got home, she found him dead drunk on the floor and his work strewn all over the place.

"Wednesday," she said, bending over to pick up his empty whiskey glass on the coffee table, along with the empty bottle beside it. "Recycling."

She made a quick sweep of their house, picking up newspapers and magazines, stopping to check whether or not he had dog-eared an article for her to clip for him to read at a later time. She found magazines he had read that morning on the floor by his desk in the study. There was one article he had dog-eared on black holes, another on intensive French gardening, and a third that was a book review in the *Times* on the history of economic development in Peru by someone he believed to be his academic rival.

Her husband had once been passionate about Peru, ancient Peru. Oddly, they had never gone to Peru because he was afraid of flying. He had also once been passionate about gardening. The interest in black holes was new.

She clipped the three articles, carefully noted the date in the upper right hand corner, and placed them on the top of the stack of articles that covered his big wooden desk in his study.

"Vince called me at work and suggested we join him and Dianna for dinner this evening. Thought it might do us all a little good to get out. He suggested something cheap and easy, Chinese maybe. But, I told him we couldn't join them because you'd gone off Chinese since you'd read that article about MSG. Plus, I thought we could stay home and have a salad with a little bread and cheese. It's too damn hot to cook."

He didn't stir. It didn't surprise her. She actually didn't expect him to stir. These days it usually took an hour or so of her stomping around the place, picking up whatever it was he had thrown about during one of his drunken afternoon tantrums, before he came to.

Eventually he'd wake up and it would be like it had always been between the two of them: neither one of them would say anything about the empty bottles or what he had done during the day. They'd play it light and easy.

They never talked about anything ugly. That wasn't their style. There had only been that one time, five years ago, when the drinking and the pills had gotten so bad that a student had come screaming into the Academic Dean's office complaining he wasn't learning anything because Daniel was too drunk to speak.

The incident didn't seem to bother Daniel as much as the fact that, afterwards, his TA, not he, had been asked by the Dean to elaborate on what might be happening or not happening in the classroom. The TA, for God's-sake.

"Like it was some big secret that I drank," he told her, throwing one unread book after another across the room, watching it splat against the wall, then tumble down to the floor in a heap of thrown books. "Sons of bitches."

He was drunk the first time she met him. Drunker than anyone she had ever known in her life. Drunk, but brilliant. Brilliantly drunk.

They were at a party at a mutual friend's house. It was a beautiful spring day and the party had spilled out into the backyard. Daniel was standing in the middle of the yard, a drink in his hand, holding court as though he was a professor in front of a classroom: talking about ancient Peru, about religion, about how maps not only represented the world but also represented the way we thought about the world. There was a child's sandbox in the backyard. He handed Eleanor his drink and bent down in order to smooth the sand with the palm of his hand and to remove all the toys.

When everything was cleared away, he picked up a stick and began to draw the map of the world. Once he finished, he made Eleanor walk around the flat circular map he had meticulously and accurately drawn across the breadth of the sandbox challenging her to name each place his stick touched.

He was the teacher, she, now, his student. She took the challenge and began answering his questions in rapid fire. The rest of the crowd dispersed.

She knew all but the Indian Ocean. He wasn't impressed. Drink in hand, Daniel rattled off capitals and rivers, history and facts. He made her draw in the equator, guiding her hand as she pulled the stick along the sand. He forced her to get down on her knees and peer at the world from the South Pole, then crawl up to the top of the map and peer down from the North.

"Notice something?" he asked as she bent low to look towards the equator from the North Pole after looking first from the South.

What she noticed was that his voice was soft and warm. She trusted him. She felt like he was going to show her some wonderful truth about the world that was going to change her life forever. She held her breath.

He didn't wait for her to answer.

"Here's my theory," he told her, leaning close to her as he squinted his eyes looking down from the North Pole over her shoulder to the equator and beyond to the South Pole. "Our childish belief in Santa Claus has shaped, no warped, our world view."

"Yes," she said, looking hard down the deeply drawn lines.

"Exactly. When you look at the world, I mean, really look at the world, you can easily see that Central and South America are much bigger than North America. Much. But that's not what we believe. We believe that North America is bigger: not only bigger, but also better and smarter. That's because Santa Claus lives at the North Pole. Santa Claus is bigger and better than almost anything else in most of our lives. He IS the North Pole. This makes the North Pole the TOP of the world while the South Pole is the BOTTOM. We all know that if you're on top, you're bigger and stronger and better than anything on the bottom. By virtue of Santa Claus, we have the winning team. We're Varsity and everything below the equator is merely puny and JV. If Santa Claus lived at the South Pole, our world would be turned upside down."

Eleanor looked at Daniel's still body lying uncomfortably on the floor.

"I'm going to go start dinner now," she announced.

She straightened the cushions on the couch, picked up the television remote and clicked down the volume. She thought of turning it off altogether but knew he slept better with it on. She was hoping he would sleep off the booze and be lucid at dinner. She needed him to be sitting up straight and listening.

Vince had pushed her a little harder than usual when he had called about dinner. When she had begged off saying Daniel had a touch of the flu, Vince said it was about time she did something about the drinking. He said it was her responsibility, as his wife, to make him stop killing himself. If you don't want to or can't, he said, then leave him.

She knew he was right. Staying didn't fix anything. In fact, it made it easier for Daniel. She was good at covering for him. Too good.

She told Vince she had decided to leave Daniel and that the real reason they couldn't come to dinner was that she planned to tell him this evening.

"Dinner, just the two of us," she said, walking into the room again hoping Daniel would hear her this time. "Something easy. I'm thinking about making a pitcher of sweet tea. Maybe eating on the porch. I'll put out the citronella candles to get rid of the bugs. Sound good?"

When he didn't stir at the promise of sweet tea, one of his favorite non-alcoholic drinks, she decided to let him sleep. She wanted to go out to the garden and get a sprig or two of fresh mint to simmer with the tea. She'd noticed the other day that the marigolds were in bloom in the garden. There was time, with Daniel still sleeping, to pick a big bouquet for the table. She wanted to make it nice, if not friendly.

The garden was a big tangled mess. It was Daniel's garden, and like most of his projects it had gotten out of hand. Raspberry canes had been allowed to grow at random, sending runners everywhere, creating a kind of barbed-wire fence both around and through the yard, which was the garden. They had no lawn.

Lawns, Daniel loudly declared to anyone who would listen, were the physical embodiment of all that was satanic and suburban. As he put it, grass that was not eaten by animals was the non-productive, scorching, water-sucking scourge of the earth.

Eleanor carefully pushed a prickly stalk of raspberry cane aside and stepped into the center of the garden. The lettuce had bolted in the heat as had most of the herbs, and it looked like it had been weeks since Daniel had been outside long enough to pinch the suckers off the tomatoes. It would not be a good harvest.

Eleanor stepped gingerly across the garden. There were lumpy piles of rotting leaves and compost everywhere. Their stench filled the air. Daniel believed seriously in compost.

Eleanor slid her garden sheers into her pants pocket and began pinching the tomato suckers. She forgot about the mint she had come to get and the tea she had wanted to make and began working her way down the row, pinching and tossing the tender green tops onto the various piles of compost around her feet. Daniel had put in more than thirty tomato plants in the spring. This rash act of planting had been caused by an article he had read about an outbreak of botulism in hothouse tomatoes.

After reading the article, he had forbidden Eleanor to purchase any tomatoes anywhere. He said the grocery stores bloody lied about "field grown" tomatoes, and that for sure you couldn't trust what the vendors said at the farmer's markets.

If she wanted a real tomato for a salad or a sandwich, all she would need to do was step out into their garden and pick one.

LEAVING

The rest of the garden was an odd assortment of vegetables Daniel had read about in this gourmet cookbook or other. They had kohlrabi, long white daikon radishes, bokchoy cabbage, fennel bulbs, New Zealand hot weather spinach with pungent leathery leaves, and a dozen other things that Eleanor had no idea how to cook.

For the most part, Daniel planted, then Daniel ignored. Eleanor was grateful he had once read that hot peppers and marigolds were natural pesticides, so the garden was at least wild with color.

She carefully selected a dozen or more giant yellow marigolds, cutting the stems close to where they branched so other flowers would come along behind them, and a half dozen or so stems of the bright orange and red chili peppers. Daniel didn't like it when she cut the flowers and peppers from the garden, but there were so many, she doubted a few would either be missed or change Daniel's delicate ecosystem of the garden's pest control.

She took another quick pass through the tomatoes, plucking two firm red ones the size of baseballs. She rummaged through the herbs pinching a few bits here and there. She found a bunch of flat leafed Italian parsley, a soft green twig of oregano and a fistful of sweet basil. She'd crush these together with a little olive oil and lemon juice for the salad dressing.

Fireflies were beginning to dance and flitter through the garden. She heard the streetlight on the corner click on. She looked at her watch. It was nearly 8 o'clock. Daniel was usually sullen when she didn't get dinner on the table before 8:30 p.m.. He believed that eating past a certain hour gave him indigestion and made sleep impossible.

When she got into the kitchen, she quickly rinsed the fistful of herbs she'd cut and put them in a bowl. Then she trimmed the stems of the marigolds and peppers and arranged them in a lovely ceramic vase she'd bought last week at a yard sale.

"Got two tomatoes from the garden for our salad," she called out.

She opened the fridge and grabbed a bag of mixed greens from the crisper, rinsed them and dumped them into the wooden salad bowl. She chopped the tomato and the half of a cucumber left over from last night.

She found a small piece of Gorgonzola, an over ripe Brie and a few slices of prosciutto. She arranged these on a platter along with the bread. She carried the platter, two plates, their silverware and two glasses filled with ice out to the porch. That's when she realized she'd forgotten to start the tea.

"Eighty-six on the tea," she called out cheerily. "I've got some seltzer and raspberry syrup. I can make you one of those I-tal-lian sodas you like."

She swung her head around the doorway. Daniel hadn't moved. He was still where she'd found him when she had come home from work.

"Okay, Dr. Daniel, it's dinnertime."

She came into the room and stooped down beside him. She reached out to touch his shoulder.

"Wake up," she shouted.

His body was hard and stiff against her hand. His face was cold to the touch. His eyes tightly shut.

She put her face close to his. She breathed against him. She held her breath. He didn't breathe back.

She got up from the floor and sat on the chair near the couch. She could hear the soft clicking and buzzing of June bugs crashing blindly against the porch light.

She didn't cry. Instead, she took a long deep breath. She let the breath fill her lungs. She held it until it stung and then she slowly let it out.

LEAVING

Daniel had once told her that when a body dies there's a moment when the spirit, the soul, the last breath, leaves the body and fills the room. She looked around. She held her arms out and moved her hands through the stillness of the room. It was empty.

She picked up the television remote and clicked it off. She sat back down in the chair. The room was dark and quiet. In a minute, she'd call Vince and Dianna.

She wondered when Daniel's last breath and the last bit of hope and dreams they once shared had come and gone, and how she had missed it.

PINHOLE VISION

Laura's father carefully unscrewed the blue glass finial from the top of their tallest living room lamp and slipped off the shade. The light from the bulb flooded the room. He put the lamp on the coffee table, pushed the kitchen stool in front of the table and closed the thick damask drapes so no other light could come in.

"Sit here," he told her mother pointing to the kitchen stool, "and look there, towards the wall, so I can see the outline of your face."

Laura's mother sat on the stool, careful to sit straight so her head was about even with the bare light bulb. She pulled back her hair so he could see her forehead, nose, and chin in profile against the bright light.

"Let your hair fall down to your shoulders," he said. "I want to see how long it is now. You haven't cut it have you?"

"No," she answered.

Her mother let her hands drop and tilted her chin up so her hair would fall softly against her neck.

Laura thought her mother looked like one of those beautiful Breck girls in the magazine ads. She wondered if her father knew about Breck shampoo. She also wondered how much he saw when he looked at them against the bright light of the exposed bulb.

PINHOLE VISION

Her father turned his head toward the bright light and frowned. He rubbed his eyes with the heels of his hands and walked toward the lamp.

"Sorry," he said to Laura, as he turned off the light.

Laura's mother looked to her as if to say she was sorry too, and took the stool back to the kitchen.

Laura was disappointed. It had been almost a year since the last time her father had seen her silhouette against the glare of the exposed bulb. She was seven then, but now she was eight and her hair was even longer than her mother's and she wore it in a ponytail. She was anxious for him to see how grownup she'd become.

She stood silently by as her father put the lamp back together again. She didn't offer to help, hoping he would change his mind. Laura secretly worried her father would never again have the chance to see her because he never knew when it was going to happen, how long it would last, or if it would ever happen again once it left him.

Pinhole vision is what he called it: a kind of stark explosion of images through one tiny receptor at the back of his sightless eyes that would, without warning, work for a moment, giving him the pleasure of sight. It was a pleasure, however, that often left him with a sick headache. It was a headache, Laura knew without asking, that meant no one could come to the house today to play.

Laura stepped aside so her father could go to his room to put on his dark glasses and rest.

"He was blind?" Andrew asked. The two of them were sitting in Laura's kitchen. Andrew had just asked her to marry him and he wanted her to tell him everything.

"Since birth. But you wouldn't have known it."

They had moved into the house on Gloria Street the summer before she started third grade. The house was new. The neighborhood was also new. Sprung to life, her mother used to joke, out of WWII, as though it had been commissioned by the Army and plunked down in the middle of a field of dreams.

Laura didn't know anything about the army or the War, but it seemed to her that everyone who lived in her neighborhood had come from it, except for her father and their family.

"Shhhh," she cautioned Brenda, her new neighbor, her soon to be new best friend, who had come to the door that morning to see if she could play. "My father is resting."

Laura slipped her thin body between the screen and front door, careful to hold in the tongue of the lock on the door so it wouldn't make a sound when she pulled it shut. She didn't want to wake her father.

"My mother says your father is blind," Brenda said.

"He is."

"Got shot in the face in Germany or somewhere over there."

"Born that way."

"How do you get born blind?"

"You just do."

"But he can see, can't he?"

"Nope."

"I don't believe you."

Laura took a moment before she tried to explain everything to Andrew.

"You would have had to have known him to understand," Laura said, pouring another glass of wine for herself.

PINHOLE VISION

"I want to understand," Andrew told her, gently rubbing the rim of his wine glass, round and round, until it made a slight humming noise. "I want to know everything about him and about you."

There were so many things to say. So many things she'd never talked about to anyone before.

Laura had loved growing up in their house. She loved that she could stand on their new cement front stoop, look down the block and see her school. It was big with blue doors and was named after a president, like all the other schools in this new city. Unfortunately, by the time they had built her school, the school board had already used all the more honorable presidential names like Jefferson and Roosevelt. Her school was named Taft, an easy name to remember and to spell, which pleased Laura but not her father. When her father took her to register for third grade, he told the school secretary it was a damn shame to name an elementary school after a lazy shiftless Republican like Taft.

The secretary didn't bother to look at her father in his dark glasses; instead, she looked straight at Laura and announced that Taft wasn't lazy, just fat, and it didn't matter what they called the school as long as the children learned how to read and write.

"My mother says we have to be careful when we play at your house," Brenda said.

"About what?"

"Leaving toys on the floor or not pushing our chairs in when we leave the table. She says your dad could trip over them and hurt himself."

"That's not true."

"That's what she says."

"She doesn't know."

"There was this girl," Laura said, holding the wineglass by its delicate stem in order to bring it up to the light so she could look through the dark wine to see the face of the man who wanted to marry her, who insisted he wanted to know everything about her.

"Brenda was her name and she was my best friend until she got saved in tenth grade and told me I was a heathen and she couldn't talk to me anymore.

"She had a younger brother named Jake. One day they were over at our house playing. It must have been right after Christmas or my birthday because the living room floor was littered with books and toys. We heard my father coming up the stairs from the basement. Brenda and Jake got real quiet and quit playing. I didn't know what was happening, so I quit playing too. When my father walked through the room, he stopped for a moment and said hello to both Jake and Brenda, called them by name the way anyone would. After he spoke, he continued walking to his bedroom without stepping on anything.

"As soon as he was gone, Brenda stood up and told Jake to get up too. She grabbed Jake's hand and announced they were going home because they weren't allowed to play with liars.

"Do you understand? They thought he could see because he knew who they were."

"Could he?"

"What?"

"See?"

"He was blind."

"Then how did he know who they were?"

"He just did."

PINHOLE VISION

The Weekly Readers came every Tuesday after the last recess. Mrs. Moore, her third grade teacher would put them on their desks. When they came in from recess, they were expected to sit down and begin reading the first story silently to themselves.

Laura was the last to come in one day because it was her job to hang the jump ropes on the coat hook by the door. When she slid into her seat, everyone stopped reading and looked at her.

"When everyone is done reading," Mrs. Moore intoned, "we'll discuss the story."

The students went back to reading, their heads bent down over their desks. Laura picked up her Reader and started in on the story. It was about being handicapped.

"There are all kinds of handicaps," Mrs. Moore began a few minutes later, holding the Weekly Reader out in her hand as though she too were reading it. "Can anyone name a handicap?"

"Deafness," Thomas Winters called out.

"Being crippled," added Brenda.

"What about being blind?" Mrs. Moore asked, looking straight at Laura.

"That's not a handicap," Laura said.

"But of course it is, Laura, in fact, it's probably the worst kind," Mrs. Moore said, straightening her back and looking down at Laura over the edge of the Weekly Reader she held out in front of her.

"It is NOT," Laura screamed. "It is NOT at all like being deaf or crippled."

Then she did something she often dreamed of doing but never thought she would have the courage to do: she stood up from her seat, walked to the door, and once she could see her house, she began running. She ran until she reached the cool safe surface of the cement stoop and she sat down and cried.

"What was your father like?"

"My mother used to say he was the kind of man who should have been born rich."

"Why rich?"

"Because he liked things."

"Like what?"

"Dark gray pinstriped suits with starched white shirts. Navy blue wool gabardine sports jackets."

"He liked colors?"

"And textures. Smooth felt hats. Tan cashmere coats. He always said there was something special about the feel of red silk."

"And your mother?"

"She didn't care that much about red silk, but she would wear it for my father and whenever she did he would say she looked beautiful."

Laura's father was the only father in the neighborhood who wore a white shirt to work. Dressed in a suit and tie, he would walk to his insurance office in town every morning after he walked her to school. Her mother would pick her up from school. Her father would come home every night precisely at six, just in time to wash his hands and sit down to dinner.

All the other fathers in the neighborhood worked in the automobile factories. Those who pulled the day shift left before their kids got up and came home from work when their children got home from school. If they worked afternoons, they left when school was over and came back when their kids were in bed. Brenda's father worked the night shift, so they could never play at her house because her father was always sleeping.

PINHOLE VISION

Brenda's father wore blue pants and blue work shirts to the factory and his hands were big and rough. On his days off he fixed things in their garage. Laura's father's hands were smooth. He didn't fix things. He sat in the living room and listened to the news on the radio or put on his earphones and listened to Talking Books.

Sometimes, her father would go outside after dinner to mow their lawn, pulling their small gas mower behind him, kicking his feet as he walked in order to know he was pulling the mower across uncut grass.

Once, when Brenda's father was out in the backyard and her own father was mowing the lawn, Laura saw Brenda's father look over at her father then look away as though there were something shameful about a man who had to drag a mower behind him rather than push it in front of him like someone who could see.

"Sometimes Mom would go out to dinner with her friends. She was very different from Dad. She liked to be in the middle of things. She liked to gossip, to be with people, to dance at parties.

"It was funny. Everyone called my mom by her first name. Even the kids in the neighborhood called her Linda. But they didn't call my father by his first name; it was as though he didn't have a first name. Everyone called him Mr. Beckman. My mom would call him Mr. Beckman when she was annoyed at something he'd done or said and she didn't want to fight, instead, just wanted to warn him she was getting agitated.

"When she'd go out with her friends, Dad and I would walk into town and have dinner at this little restaurant not far from his office.

"One night, a new waitress seated us and gave both of us menus. When she came back to take the order she looked at my father. When she saw he was wearing dark glasses she looked away from him and turned to me to ask what he wanted.

"I told her she should ask him. My father pretended nothing had happened and gave her his order. After both of us had placed our orders, Dad asked for a cup of coffee. Again, the waitress turned to me and asked whether he wanted cream and sugar. I exploded. He's blind, I told her, not deaf and dumb.

"We never talked about him being blind at home, and I knew what I had said was ugly. It felt ugly in my mouth the way things that you shouldn't say do. I thought my father was going to be angry with me. Instead he laughed this great big laugh. His laughter filled the restaurant. Everyone quit talking and stared at us. The waitress was so embarrassed, she took off her apron and left."

"What happened next?"

"The owner brought us our food and apologized. He said the waitress was new and didn't know. My father just waved his hand as if to say it was nothing to worry about.

"After dinner, when we were walking back home, my father told me that people who couldn't talk weren't dumb. They were mute, and that he didn't want me to ever use the word dumb again."

When Laura was in high school, she'd go to her father's office on Saturdays in order to help him write letters or file. When her father talked to people on the phone about their insurance policies, he took notes in Braille. Afterwards, he'd call his secretary into his office and he'd read his notes to her and she would fill out the policies or make any changes he had noted. He kept his Braille notes on all his customers in his desk, and the secretary kept her written ones in the files in the front office.

The work seemed simple enough and it made Laura mad that people were always so amazed a blind person could sell insurance, as if it was some kind of miracle a blind person could do anything but eat and sleep.

Bobby Davis was the first boy who ever asked Laura out, and from the minute he picked her up for their date, he couldn't quit asking questions about her father. He wanted to know why he was blind, and what he did all day. He said he couldn't imagine what it would be like to be blind and not be able to do anything.

They had gone to a school dance but neither one of them was comfortable dancing, so they had come home early and were sitting in Bobby's dad's car in front of Laura's house talking.

The windows were beginning to get steamed up and Laura was wondering just how long they could sit in the car before her dad would come out to ask what was going on. She wished Bobby would just shut up about her father.

"Does he work?" Bobby asked.

"He owns an insurance company," she told him.

"I don't believe he sells insurance." Bobby said, sure that he had caught her in a lie.

"You're right," she told him. "He doesn't. He robs banks."

"But he's blind."

"Who says?" Laura taunted.

"Everyone. He wears dark glasses."

"Part of his disguise. That and the insurance company. Do you really think the police are going to arrest a blind man for robbing a bank?"

"Maybe not."

"That's how he gets away with it. No one can believe it's true."

Andrew poured himself another glass of wine and topped off Laura's glass.

"What kinds of things did he like to do?" he asked.

"He loved the movies. Westerns, murder mysteries, espionage, James Bond, anything but stupid things where they took fairy tales and messed them up. He didn't care too much for romantic comedies either, except those wonderful Spencer Tracy and Katherine Hepburn ones. Those were the best. My mom had no patience with the movies. She said she couldn't sit still long enough to watch a movie. She liked to do things and go places, anything but sit still.

"My dad and I would go to the weekend matinees when the place was full of kids. We'd sit in the back row. All the kids would be piled up in the front and they'd be laughing and talking, and my father could get the feel of what was going on from their chatter.

"Sometimes, there'd be this long silence in the movies, especially in the westerns, where two guys were facing off getting ready to draw. The audience would be holding its breath. My dad would touch my arm and I'd tell him what was going on.

"It was the only time I was his eyes and the two of us needed each other."

Laura didn't know what to tell people when her parents divorced. Her best friend Brenda was shocked and said she couldn't imagine how a blind man could leave his wife and live on his own. Laura said blindness had nothing to do with it.

But she had lied. For a long time before the divorce, her father didn't do anything when he was home but sit in his chair with his earphones on while her mother went on about her business as though no one was in the house. Laura wasn't sure what was wrong, but she knew the air was electrified the way it often is when a storm is coming and you can feel it on your skin long before you see it come washing across the horizon.

"Are you like your dad?" Andrew asked.

"I'm like my mother in that I can see, but more like my father in how I feel about things."

Laura didn't like her father's earphones any more than her mother did, but they were a necessary evil of his desire to read and keep up with the world by listening to Talking Books. The earphones, however, shut the two of them out of his world. If he didn't wear them when he wanted to read, they had to listen to his books too, which was like having someone read aloud while you tried to vacuum, take a shower, read your own book or newspaper, or talk on the phone.

Laura knew the earphones were only part of it. The real problem was that her mother had wanted a job and her father didn't want her to have one. Whenever the subject came up, he refused to talk about it, saying he made plenty of money and he didn't see why she needed to make more.

She said she wanted to get out of the house. She said she felt like a prisoner. She said she wanted her own life.

Laura could hear them after she went to bed each night. They would usually start talking in one room, then move to another. It was as if they were searching for a place where they could feel comfortable talking to each other. Eventually the talk would turn into a fight, and her mother would slam their bedroom door, and her father would go into the living room and put on his earphones and sit in his chair. The next morning, Laura would find her father asleep in his chair and her mother in the kitchen making coffee as though nothing had happened.

It all ended abruptly the afternoon her mother came home with a department store name badge in her purse.

"You can't do this to me," her father had said, refusing to sit at the dinner table.

"Do what to you?"

"Embarrass me like this. Make people think I can't provide for you and Laura."

"Who cares what people think?" her mother argued.

"I'm blind."

"And, I'm not."

It was over before their dinner got cold. He was gone and her mother cleared the dishes and went to her room and shut the door.

"I would go to my father's office on my way home from school everyday. On Friday afternoon, he'd give me my allowance. We'd talk. Sometimes I'd answer the phone for him.

"He had an apartment near the movie theatre. We'd go to the movies together on weekends just like we always had. When I was in college, I'd come home for the holidays and we'd go to the movies every day. We had this deal where we'd save up movies to go to together. I'd call him and say save this one for me. He'd agree and ask me to save some other one for him. We'd have a list and we would see them all: musicals, mysteries, comedies, and even those horrible things Disney made. *Fantasia* was the worst for my father. Nice music, but nothing about *Fantasia* made any sense to him.

"I used to think that if my mother would have gone to the movies with us, she would have stayed with him."

Andrew leaned his arms on the table and looked at her straight on as though she might bolt and run.

"You're not your mother and I'm not your father," he said.

Laura reached behind her and turned off the light.

"And then what happened?" he asked.

PINHOLE VISION

"And then he died. Just like that. One minute he was walking down the street talking with a friend, and the next minute he was dead. A heart attack. My mother was the one who called to tell me.

"I didn't know what to say to her. I was still angry she'd left him. I felt so empty and strange, like he'd never even been in my life."

"Was he handsome?"

"Like a god."

Slowly, Laura began to talk in the dark. She told him about her parents fighting during the night and how she couldn't go to sleep until it was over and she heard her father walk to the living room to sit in his chair and her mother slam the bedroom door. She told him about the time she told Bobby Davis her father was a bank robber. And about Mrs. Moore and that stupid third grade Weekly Reader and how she ran home and cried on the front porch wishing her father would be the one to find her and take her back to school so she could show Mrs. Moore he wasn't handicapped. But, instead, it was her mother who came home and found her, washed her face, and took her back to school.

When Andrew reached across the table and took her hand, Laura was surprised at how cool his fingers felt against her skin. All at once she remembered how it was to sit next to her father in the movies and to tell him about the things he couldn't see. Then, she told Andrew the truth about her father.

"Sometimes he could see. Not for long, and not very well, but he could see. He called it pinhole vision. Whenever it happened, he would take the lampshade off the big table lamp in the living room and put my mother on a chair in front of it. And, if she sat very still, he could see her, an image of her, against the bright light for just a moment. Then the vision would be gone and he would be blind again."

THE BLACK SIAMESE TWINS
MEET QUEEN VICTORIA

Celine and Louisa May were born within hours of Prince Albert's death on December 14, 1861. They would have died, too, had their mother, Mattie Hinton, not been employed by the Thomas H. Wilcox family of London.

Mattie's water broke at 4 in the morning, bathing her legs with water and blood. She woke her husband.

"Get the mister," she cried, pushing Horace away from her. "Go now. I'm in trouble, oh Lord, I'm in trouble." Then she rolled and cried, her nightgown slapped against her great body like a wet sail tangled on a mast. Horace sprang from the room, and ran through the silent house to wake Mr. Wilcox.

When Mr. Wilcox came to the doorway of Mattie's room, Mrs. Wilcox standing beside him with a light raised over her head, there was blood all over the bed and floor.

"You've gotta get your brother," Mattie cried out, "Please, Mr. Wilcox, my babies are in trouble. Please help me. They're gonna die."

"Hush now, Mattie," Mrs. Wilcox said, coming into the room behind her husband. "There's only one baby in there, and it's going to be fine. Horace, get the fire in the stove lit, and bring me Mr. Wilcox's whiskey. Thomas, go fetch your brother."

THE BLACK SIAMESE TWINS MEET QUEEN VICTORIA

Mr. Wilcox was back with his brother in less than half an hour. When Dr. John Wilcox came into the room he didn't like what he saw. "There's a procedure," he said, talking softly to Mattie in a slow, even voice, "where you cut along the line where the baby lies, then lift the baby from the womb."

Anna Wilcox felt faint, but held her balance, bracing her knee against the edge of Mattie's bed.

"Horace, hold Mattie's hands and shoulders," said John Wilcox. "Thomas, her legs and feet. I'm going to make the incision and try my best to keep her from bleeding too much. When I tell you to reach in and grab the baby, Anna, you do it. But first, give Mattie some whiskey."

The four of them stood in amazement as, minutes later, Anna Wilcox reached her small white hands into the thick, bloody body of Mattie Hinton and pulled out two tiny joined twins no bigger than a leg of lamb or one of Mattie's double-layer fresh coconut cakes.

"Twins, Siamese twins," John Wilcox gasped, grabbing the head of the second one in order to help Anna keep from dropping them.

"Give her another drink of whiskey, Horace. Tom, let go of her legs, reach into the babies' mouths, clear them of mucus. Anna, tip them upside down. Are they breathing?"

No one moved. "Are they breathing?" he screamed, then grabbed the babies from Anna's hands. "Breathe," he commanded the small tangled babies. "Breathe!"

And they did, their mouths opening and closing as they gulped air. He grabbed a blanket from the end of the bed and wrapped the babies in it, then carried them to the kitchen. He held them tightly, cradling them against his chest while he used his body to push Mattie's worktable next to the warm stove.

The babies stopped crying when he laid them down. As he unwound the blanket, he could see exactly how they were joined: at the shoulder and hip. With two such joins, more than likely, they could not be detached. However, since they were joined side by side, and not facing each other, they probably did not share any vital organs, which meant they could survive together.

He touched the web of flesh between them. The baby on the right seemed more whole than the other. She had two full arms and two full legs. But the baby on the left was slightly malformed: her left arm, the one that was attached at the shoulder to her sister's arm, hung lifeless against her sister's body, and her left leg ended abruptly in a curved foot, as though the other sister had always been stronger, pushing against the other, crowding her in the womb. He believed the foot could be corrected. He thought the girls were beautiful.

He covered them with the blanket then rummaged through the kitchen searching for a clean cloth. When he found one, he dipped it into the basin of water still heating on the stove, wrung it out, and began bathing the babies. They screamed and wiggled, turning their heads from side to side. He found a second clean cloth and dipped it into a cup of milk, and stuck it in the first baby's mouth.

The baby sucked. If they were to live he was going to have to get Mattie to feed them. He dipped the other end of the cloth into the milk and gave it to the second baby.

They had to live. He finished washing them, brushing the wet rag against the curled hair on their heads. Their skin was the color of pecans, their hair black and soft as torn wet silk. He wrapped the blanket around their legs and arms, swaddling them as best he could. As far as he knew, these were the only two living black Siamese twins on Earth.

He dipped his fingers into the pot of warm water.

"I baptize you Celine," he said to the first, crossing her forehead with his wet fingers, "and you, little one-arm, Louisa May."

Then he took the girls and carried them back into Mattie's room.

"Here are your babies. I have baptized them. The first one, the one on the right, I baptized Celine; the other, Louisa May, after my own grandmother. You must promise to feed them and care for them. They are a special gift from God."

They were nearly two before they learned to crawl. Celine, always the faster and more coordinated, moved too quickly for Louisa May, causing them to tumble and tangle rather than move with ease from place to place. Louisa May was unbalanced by her shriveled arm, which lay lifeless by her side. It took time for her to learn to lean into her sister, allowing Celine to carry the center weight for the two of them when they moved.

The doctor was impressed by their general good health and development. He came by every week to check on them, sometimes taking them in his carriage to the hospital, where he could watch them more closely and chart their progress. There were also times when he took them to other physicians, asking what should be done about Louisa May's arm and foot.

He had thought at first that Louisa May's arm should be removed. He feared, as the two girls grew, their bodies would drain off the small blood supply that pulsed through her crippled arm, strangulating it and endangering both of their lives.

But he didn't know. He just didn't know why that arm was there or why it wasn't whole. He also didn't know what would happen to either Louisa May or Celine if it were gone.

When they were old enough to talk, they called him Dr. John. By then they were almost as much a part of him as they were part of each other. He took them to the major hospitals and medical schools in London, introducing them to other doctors who wanted to see and touch the strange, dark purple joins that entangled their two lives.

When they were six, he took them to Paris to the Academy of Physicians. The evening before they were to go before the conference to be examined, Dr. John was awakened in the middle of the night by the terrified screams of Louisa May. When he entered their room, he found Celine trying to hold Louisa May's head with her free arm, rocking her sobbing sister gently from side to side.

"Louisa May, why are you crying?"

"Please don't let them touch me anymore. Please, their fingers hurt like knives. I don't want them to cut me. I don't want them to see me. Don't let them cut off my arm."

While Louisa May cried, Celine remained silent.

"I won't let them take off your arm. I promise you," Dr. John said.

"Don't let them touch me."

"They're doctors, Louisa May. They won't hurt you. They want to help you. Do you remember how Dr. Alexander helped your foot? You can walk more easily now, you and Celine, because he was able to fix your foot. Celine isn't crying. She knows they won't hurt you. Don't you, Celine?"

But the other girl didn't speak; she held fast to her sister's head, rocking back and forth, just as she had done when he first came into the room.

"Go back to sleep. No one will hurt you or cut off your arm. I promise you."

When he left the room he closed the door then stood in the hall for a long time listening to Louisa May cry. His heart was pounding. He was as frightened by Celine's silence as he was by Louisa May's tears.

THE BLACK SIAMESE TWINS MEET QUEEN VICTORIA

He did not understand why the two of them were joined any more than he understood what it must be like for them to be so connected.

He thought about the day when they were born, and how before he even washed the blood from their bodies or offered them their first taste of milk, he reached to touch the mysterious skin where their lives met.

Edward Henry made his way into London society by gambling. He was handsome. His father had been white, so he was fair and his hair was soft to the touch. He was proud of his silky black hair and wore it smoothed back, with no part. When he took off his hat, his waves seemed to fall and ripple from the top of his head to the tip of his ears.

He had his mother's straight nose and full mouth, which always seemed to smile yet told nothing. He was good at cards and never swore or carried a pistol. His father had not married his mother, but gave her a small ruby stickpin on the day he was born. Edward wore it for luck.

When he first came to London to gamble, he was invited only into back rooms where green-felt tables greeted his soft tan hands and quick shuffle. Then, as the stakes grew, along with his reputation as both a gentleman and a gambler, he made his way into the most fashionable homes and front parlors of Queen Victoria's London.

Dr. John's brother, Thomas Wilcox, was also a gambler. He got lucky sometimes, but he mostly played for sport. And, if he lost a little money now and then, it never seemed to matter.

It was late one Saturday night, in the Wilcox's front parlor, that Edward Henry first saw the twins. It had been a good night for him at the table. The company was rich, refined and eager to play. He had moved cautiously at first, since this was the first time Mr. Wilcox had asked him into his home. He played his cards close the first few hands, playing only to get the feel of how important it might be for Wilcox to win. He knew there was money in the room and that he could make it now or later. It didn't matter to him; all that mattered was getting invited back.

They had played for several hours before Mr. Wilcox stood up and pulled the cord near the double doors, ringing for the servants to bring whiskey and refreshments. It was past midnight and the room was filled with the stale, sweet smell of cigars and cherry tobacco smoke.

Mattie came into the room pushing a teacart laden with cold roast beef and ham sandwiches. The twins came in behind her, carrying a tray of fresh glasses and whiskey. Edward Henry was startled by the way they moved, their shoulders so tight they must be touching.

He had heard about the girls, as had everyone in London, yet, when he saw them walk into the room, he forgot they were joined. When Celine put down the silver tray, and Louisa May, the thick-cut crystal decanter, he saw the shortened arm of the one hanging lifeless against the full arm of her sister.

Looking more closely, he could see their black skirts were sewn together about six inches from their waists. It made them look as though they were ballerinas whose long gowns meshed as one in their movement, allowing them to float instead of walk, one beside the other.

As they came close to Edward Henry in order to replace the dirty glasses at the table with fresh ones, he tipped his head to the ladies and smiled at them. Louisa May turned her face away. Celine, on the other hand, stood firm, almost defiant, meeting his glance.

They didn't speak. Within minutes the twins and Mattie were gone and the game resumed. Edward Henry chose to lose the next few hands, allowing Thomas Wilcox the pleasure of winning in front of his friends.

When the game was over, Edward pushed himself away from the table. "You've taken quite enough from me tonight," he said, preparing to go.

"Fascinating, aren't they?" Mr. Wilcox asked.

"Pardon?"

"I was talking about the twins. I believe you smiled at them. You know, it's rare to see a gambler let down his guard. Almost as rare as seeing a pair of black Siamese twins. Don't you agree?"

"I apologize, I meant them no disrespect or harm."

"Surely."

"Which one is Celine?"

"The one that stood firm. I was busy and didn't see what happened. However, I can guess that Celine stared back when you looked at her. She's a fighter. The other, Louisa May, is more withdrawn. Knowing the two as I do, I'd wager Louisa May turned her head when you looked at them."

"She wouldn't make much of a gambler, would she?"

"No," replied Thomas Wilcox, wondering just how much of a gambler this young man really was and how much he would be willing to lose.

"Does anyone call on them?" Edward asked.

"Are you interested?"

"I could be," Edward said.

"It's none of my affair. Their parents work for me. The twins live here. If you call on them, it's your business. I'm sure I have them to thank for my good fortune at the table tonight. Good night, Mr. Henry."

Edward Henry sent a driver around the next day with flowers; two nosegays of violets and baby's breath.

Carrie Jane Knowles

A week passed and then another before he came one afternoon to knock at Mattie's kitchen door and ask if he could meet the twins.

"They're sixteen," she said, looking at his soft velvet lapels, the gold and ruby pin stuck through his silk tie. "The mister already told me about you. I know you're a gambler, and that you let him win the other night. He said you was good, but I don't know what that means. It's not for me to say who sees them. You need to talk to their father. He's the butler. Go round to the front door if you want to ask permission. That's where you'll find him."

Edward Henry did as Mattie said. He rang the bell on the front door and stood, gloves in hand, waiting. When Horace Hinton opened the door, Edward Henry tipped his hat and extended his hand. Horace Hinton didn't move.

"Mr. Hinton, I'd like to introduce myself. I'm Edward Henry."

"I know who you are, and I know what you want."

"I want," Edward said, "to have the pleasure of meeting your charming daughters."

"Celine, she's the one who wants to see you. Louisa May, she's different. She doesn't want anybody looking at her . . . or touching. If you hurt them, either one of them, I'll kill you."

"Louisa May," Celine said as she helped her sister hook the buttons on her left shoe, "I love him. I don't want to hurt you, but I love him. I got a right to live my own life. Just because we're attached doesn't mean we can't live. We're living. Can't you feel it? We're alive, the blood is running through our veins and we're alive."

"Whose blood? Whose veins? If you marry him, then what kind of life am I going to have?"

"We'll take care of you. You heard what he said the other night. He promised he'd take care of both of us."

184

"And when he's kissing you. What do I do then? Lie helpless at your side like my dead arm? Should I close my eyes and pretend I don't see anything? That I don't feel my lips not being kissed?"

Celine bent forward to catch the last button and pull it through the tight leather buttonhole. They had said too much. They lived too close for harsh words. It was as if at any given minute a sharp word or careless thought could push them over some terrible edge, tearing them apart. They had to be careful.

"Do you remember that Mrs. Wilcox told us this morning that Dr. John was coming by this afternoon," Celine said, smoothing the front of her white cotton petticoat. "She said to wear the blue taffeta. He wants to take us to the hospital."

"You'll have to help me with the buttons."

"It's a pretty dress, don't you agree?"

"Yes," said Louisa May as she stood with her sister to move to the closet. It's a very pretty dress."

Celine would not make love with Edward unless Louisa May was asleep. Edward went out gambling almost every night. By the time he came home, Celine and Louisa May would be asleep. He would undress in the dark; then, before slipping into bed next to Celine, he would touch the crown of her head and carefully trace the outline of her small face with his hands. By the time his hands came together under her chin, she would open her eyes to kiss him.

Once she was awake, he would lie beside her and make love to her. He took his time, letting his hands move silently over her body, always aware of Louisa May sleeping next to her. Celine's skin was smooth and soft and invited his hands to explore. He ached to touch her back, to see the deep curve of her spine as it slipped from her delicate neck to her dark rich buttocks. But he could not ask her to turn. He could not call out her name.

Their lovemaking, like so many other things in their lives together, was silent.

The three of them lived together in a strange, strangling house of silence, Louisa May turning her head when they talked, dropping her eyes when Edward looked her way. Occasionally Celine would leave notes tucked into in his coat pockets, or folded carefully under his silk neckties in his dresser. These were the things she couldn't say, the words she couldn't cry out when they made love.

Edward felt responsible for them both. It wasn't easy for him to talk with the two of them. They were tied so closely by flesh and circumstances that they had few words left to share with him or anyone else.

When Edward and Celine were first married, he tried to find a companion for Louisa May. One night, he invited a friend, another gambler, to come to dinner with them, but the stares from the other diners put an edge on the evening. Later, in the middle of the night, he heard crying. When he woke he saw Celine was holding her sister, rocking her from side to side as though she were a small child. When he reached up to touch Celine on the shoulder to ask what was to be done, she pushed his hand away. Sensing he should leave, he slipped quietly from the bed and spent the rest of the night in the front parlor.

The next afternoon when he dressed for the evening, he found a note in his inside coat pocket: "I'm scared. Louisa May doesn't want people to stare at her. Please, no more. I wish we had a child."

Like her other notes, this one left a number of questions he would never be able to ask her: why was Celine scared? Had Louisa May's crying frightened her? Had the people in the restaurant frightened her? Who was the "we" in "I wish we had a child?"

He would never know because he couldn't ask.

But, to love Celine was also to love Louisa May. He could not separate them any better than anyone else could. When he married Celine, he had also married Louisa May, although Louisa May had not married him. Sometimes he did not understand anymore whom he had married or where Celine ended and Louisa May began.

He had wanted to ask Dr. John about children. But he didn't know what to ask. Could Celine have children of her own? What would that do to Louisa May? He wasn't a praying man but sometimes he prayed, his hand resting against the smooth, sunken belly of his sleeping wife that someday a child would come to them.

It was on one such night that he first noticed Louisa May was awake. He and Celine had just made love. He lay on top of her for a few minutes, enjoying the slow, even breathing of her coming sleep, then lazily rolled to his side. Their lovemaking had been good; he felt she had been satisfied as well as he. As Celine lay sleeping beside him, he moved his hand to rest against the warm, flat surface of her belly under her nightgown. It was then that he saw Louisa May watching him. He left his hand on Celine's belly and lowered himself down to his pillow. Louisa May had not turned away when their eyes had met.

For the next few weeks, whenever he finished making love to Celine and she had fallen asleep, he looked over at Louisa May, only to find she was watching him.

When he had first met them, he had wondered how they were different. Now he wondered if there were really two of them. They seemed one, yet he had touched only half of what was there to touch. He had never seen or touched the places where they were joined, as they were always careful to keep covered, even when they slept. He had never had the pleasure of seeing the two of them naked or bathing. For the most part, Louisa May tried to remain separate from Celine and Edward. But now he felt her stares invading his life in much the same way he had invaded hers.

It made his hands tremble. He wanted to touch her. It was as though what was his was forbidden to be his. One night after a good night of gambling, he came home to make love to Celine. The lovemaking was more passionate than usual, Celine carefully moving her hips to meet his, opening her lips to him. She couldn't cry out, but instead dug her fingers into his back, pulling him closer to her, in an attempt to smother her cries. Shortly afterward, she fell asleep, and when he moved to free himself from her arms, he saw Louisa May crying.

She was silent in her cries, tears rolling to the side of her face, her mouth frozen. Before he rolled away from Celine, he reached over and touched Louisa May's full lips. She did not pull her face away. Assured she would not cry out, he let his hand trace the full line of her mouth and her chin.

His body stirred. He wanted to touch her breasts. He wanted to kiss the tears on her face, and let his mouth taste every inch of her body.

He took his hand away, then rolled back to Celine's side. His wife was sleeping. Her breathing was smooth and even. He let his hand trace the outline of her arm, resting for a moment at her hand. She did not move.

It was late. The room was dark. He wanted to whisper something to Louisa May. He wanted to tell her he loved her, but he couldn't. Instead, he moved to her side of the bed and lifted the covers, touching the soft outline of her breasts, letting his hand make love to her while she lay in silence.

Louisa May had felt the small life turning within her like a butterfly a few weeks before. It was a strange commotion that rumbled and roared within her ears. No one else could hear it.

It was the first time in all her nineteen years she had ever felt apart from Celine.

She loved the little rippling motion that spun her body away from her sister. She closed her eyes when it came, shutting out what few remaining pieces of the world were attached to her flesh. Her skin felt new and fresh.

She dreamed one night that the baby within her was whole. Perfectly whole, and his flesh was smooth and cocoa-colored. The dream was so wonderful she hated to wake herself in the morning, and began pulling against her sister's insistent pushing and prodding. She didn't want to be up and going. The baby wrestling within her was wearing her out. She needed to sleep and bathe her eyes in the luxury of her baby's sweet dreams.

"We need to go see Dr. John," Celine said, shaking her sister. "There's something wrong with you, I can feel it. It scares me, Louisa May. Please get up."

Louisa May kept her eyes closed, fighting back a wave of nausea and fear. She didn't want to see Dr. John. For the moment, she just wanted to lay still and listen to the rushing noise made by the beating of their two hearts. She pulled her shoulder away from Celine, hoping to tear her crippled arm from her sister's flesh.

"Louisa May," Celine screamed, "talk to me! Tell me what's happening to you."

Louisa May knew she couldn't let Dr, John be the one to tell Celine; she would have to tell her herself. She could feel her sister's warm, thick arm surrounding her shoulders, her breath whistling through her matted hair.

She used her good arm to steady herself and pull away from her sister's grasp. She looked down at her sister's full arms and hands and marveled at how beautiful they were. "I love you, Celine," she said. "I'm pregnant."

Celine looked away, biting her lip to keep from crying out in pain. She would run if she could, but she couldn't, so she sat, her head and shoulders turned as far away as she could turn them. If she'd had a knife, she would have cut herself free from her sister, but she had no knife. She could feel the flesh where their bodies joined burn with the strain of Louisa May's pulling, then she felt her sister lean into her.

"I'm sorry, Celine," Louisa May whispered. "I'm sorry."

"The Queen would like to meet you." Dr. John spoke as he walked into the room. He had a manner of looking from one to the other of the girls whenever he engaged them in conversation: playing a kind of three-way game of eye contact. When they were younger, it had made them laugh. But that was before. As he talked now, he fiddled with his waistcoat lapels, brushing away imaginary lint. He was afraid to meet Celine's gaze or to look into the dark, sad eyes of Louisa May.

"I have taken care of the arrangements. I will be accompanying you to Windsor Castle next Tuesday. I will pick you up at 9 o'clock so that we can be there in time to be instructed in the proper protocol."

He was glad Louisa May was not showing yet. It would still be a while. Also, given the unusual arrangement of their dresses because of the join at their hip, in all likelihood her pregnancy would go unnoticed for a long time. However, he had no idea what strain the pregnancy would put on the two girls, how it would affect them physically. He worried most about their hearts. He was still unsure about what internal systems they shared. He had known about Celine's wish to be pregnant and had always worried about having to deal with the various medical implications. He had never imagined Louisa May would be the one to bear a child.

"I will talk to her attendant personally and explain that you should not remain standing for any length of time. I have not told them why only that it is medically unwise for you to do so at the moment. I will not be with you in her chambers because the Queen has requested to see you alone. It goes without saying that you will answer any and all questions put before you by Her Majesty."

He had looked in all the medical journals, but had found no recorded births by Siamese twins. He would be the first physician in history ever to attend the birth both of Siamese twins and also of a child born to them. He had asked another physician to see the girls with him and to help with the birth.

"Before you go to see the Queen, I would like Dr. Jameson to examine you. It's just a precaution, but I want to be sure everything is as it should be, and that a visit such as this will not put too much strain on the two of you right now. I've asked Dr. Jameson to assist me during your pregnancy as well as the birth of your child."

As he looked down at the floor, trying to avoid making eye contact with either one of them as he spoke, he could see Louisa May's good hand nervously picking at the lace at the edge of her bodice. Celine sat stiffly upright and unmoving as he spoke.

It had always been the same: one of them sat occupied in quiet motion while the other sat braced as if to receive some sort of blow. It was as though the normal tensions pulling within a person were borne on the outside for Celine and Louisa May. If one studied how each twin sat or turned her head, one knew immediately the two sides of the coin being weighed and reviewed by them. He remembered so well, when they were five and Louisa May had to have her foot broken and set to make it straight so she could walk, it was she who sat ready to absorb whatever pain there might be, while Celine pulled at her clothes, swinging her two good feet as though she wished she could take flight for the two of them and run.

Their physical proximity was only a part of their curiosity: their uncanny oneness was a fascination for him as well. With very little discussion, the two of them had always managed their emotions as though these sprang forth from the same heart. They often saw with one set of eyes and moved with one purpose, as though they were a single being who by sheer accident bore an extra head and an extra pair of legs and arms.

Until Louisa May became pregnant, he had never before experienced a time with them in which they seemed to live so far apart.

He did not know how they would ever manage to suffer through and survive what lay ahead of them.

The Queen was smaller and less regal than they had imagined she would be, but neither Louisa May nor Celine turned her head to the other or made any comment. Later, when asked, they remarked they thought the Queen rather ordinary.

The Queen, on the other hand, found them fascinating. She hated Windsor Castle. Hated London; in fact, preferred Balmoral, but London provided her with diversions Balmoral lacked.

When the twins walked into her chambers, the Queen was surprised by their grace and ease of movement. She had heard they were beautiful, and she found them to be so. Their skin was dark honey-colored, and their eyes and hair pitch black. She believed the darker races to be more interesting in appearance than her own, but had never told anyone so. She would make a note of it in her journal.

"Which one of you is Louisa May?"

"I am, your Majesty," Louisa May said, pulling out the fullness of her skirt with her one good hand and bowing slightly.

They spent close to an hour with the Queen in her chambers. After she dismissed them, she called her servant and asked that her curtains be drawn closed in order to shut out the remaining light of the day. She wished to be left alone, she told the servant, so that she might write in her journal.

That night, after her chambermaid had turned down her covers, poured fresh water, and left, the Queen knelt upon her pillows so that she might bring herself closer to the portrait of Albert that hung above her bed.

"Oh, dear Albert, how I miss your unerring strength. If you could only have been here, my dearest Albert," she said, "you would have known what to do. If you could have seen them, you would have understood, and, as I did, would have wished to be bound together, shoulder to shoulder. But their eyes, their eyes felt so dark. I know if you had been here, you would have been able to tell me what the Queen should do to free them.

"Whenever I doubted what I should do before, you would be there telling me: act like the Queen.

"It was easy then, dear Albert, but now, without you near to direct my hand, I do not know what it is to be Queen anymore.

"If you had been here, you would have seen their beauty as well as their sadness. You would have noticed how they touched the earth like dancers, one knowing the movements of the other as though they had one soul."

Then the Queen sat down on her bed, slipping her bare feet and legs beneath her eiderdown coverlet, turning her back on the picture of her deceased husband.

"My love, my breath of life, how I wished you were here today with me again. Yet, how I knew, watching them, that when we were together there were things, so many things, that kept us apart. Since you are gone from my touch, we are closer together now than we could have ever been before.

"Oh, my sweet Albert. If I were truly Queen, great sovereign ruler of the vast British Empire, at the very least I should be able to lift my jeweled staff and cut the two bound twins asunder. And having done so, command them both to love and rejoice in their partings.

"If I were truly Queen."

John Edward Hinton Henry was born September 4, 1881. Dr. Jameson stood by, but it was John Wilcox who eased his head and shoulders out, as the baby screamed and kicked to the tears and applause of his mother.

Louisa May had labored throughout the previous night, crying out only once when the pain was so bad she couldn't keep her wits about her anymore. When Louisa May screamed, Celine reached out and took hold of her sister's trembling shoulders, cooing softly in her thick black hair: all would be well, she was there.

When at last John Edward came, Celine reached out to touch the child that was half hers and would be the only child the two of them would ever know.

"Is he whole?" Louisa May asked, watching his wet, squiggling body struggle against the firm grasp of Dr. John's massive hands.

"Yes, Louisa May, he's whole."

"Then I want to call him John. John Edward," she said.

THE BLACK SIAMESE TWINS MEET QUEEN VICTORIA

"I approve," said Dr. John. Then he held the baby out at arm's length so Louisa May would be able to take her child in her own arms.

But she would not reach out to claim him.

She looked away from the doctor to her sister. "Would you take him, Celine? Please, and hold him close to me so I can touch his face."

The birth left both Louisa May and Celine weakened. It was hard for Dr. John and the other physicians to explain, but the consensus was that somehow the two of them shared more than a common space on earth. More than likely, they shared the same circulatory system, and the birth pushed it beyond its strength.

Mattie took John Edward to the park on most afternoons. It was a special time for her because he was the normal baby she never had. She could take him anywhere, and no one would stare as though she had done something wrong.

Following the birth of his son, Edward Henry learned to move more silently through his house. He was afraid of the words that had never been spoken among the three of them. But he gloried nonetheless in their little boy and encouraged him, as Celine and Louisa May did, to think of them as his Mother Louisa and his Mother Celine.

When the spring came, Edward Henry took his two women out one day to watch John play with his grandmother in the park. They didn't get down from the carriage, but sat, a lap robe hiding their joined skirts, watching their child from a distance. It was a glorious day. The air was fresh and warm, and the leaves on the trees bright green in their spring budding, while mustard-colored crocuses sprang forth along the footpath, lighting the way through the park.

Edward Henry tried at that time to tell them both how much he loved them, but he couldn't find the words, or the space within their silences for him to speak.

They would die the next fall from pneumonia. Dr. John would leave their hospital room just minutes before Celine's death, leaving Louisa May to wait in solitude for her own life to end.

"Do you remember when we saw the Queen?" Louisa May asked, staring at the wide, blank ceiling of their room. "She was rather ordinary and not at all regal like I thought she should be. Don't you agree?" She prattled on, feeling the unfamiliar single beating of her heart against her chest. "You were so brave then, Celine. Answering her questions, speaking for both of us, knowing all the time I had another life that was not yours inside of me.

"Celine, my dear sweet Celine, why have you left me? Why aren't you here when I need so much to tell you that he loved you? Edward really loved you. I could see it in his eyes when he touched you. We didn't mean to hurt you. I meant to tell you so many times. I wish I had told you. I'm sorry, Celine. I wish I had told you."

APRICOTS IN A TURKISH GARDEN

"I really don't want to write about Turkey," Jim said, running his finger around the thin rim of his tea glass. The waiter came to the table and stood by silently, waiting to see if he wanted a refill. "Yes, please," he said, without looking up.

The noon rush of diners was dwindling and the hum of the restaurant had slowed to a leisurely pace, not unlike the pace of life they experienced in Istanbul. The waiter first filled Jim's glass, then Lisa's, pulling the hot teapot high into the air as he ceremoniously poured the dark liquid without missing the cup or spilling a drop. When the waiter finished, he went on to the next table.

Lisa took two large lumps of sugar from the bowl on the table and slowly stirred them into her hot tea with the small silver teaspoon, watching the sugar cube dissolve in a swirl.

"I didn't ask," she said.

"But you, like them, expect me to," he answered

"Can't you write about something?" she asked.

"Nada. Not a thing."

"Maybe they don't expect you to…"

"I'm a journalist. Everyone expects me to write about them."

"I don't," she said.

"You don't count."

"As your wife, I am personally grateful that you have never written about having lunch with me."

"Who says I haven't?"

"I would prefer to remain blissfully ignorant about when and where if you have, okay? Unless you've made me taller and thinner and a bit younger than I really am."

"I'll try to remember that in the future."

"I was happy they asked you to come along on the trip to Turkey. Otherwise, it would have been a long two weeks without you. Would you have preferred that? Time alone?"

"It's not that," he said, taking a careful sip of his hot tea.

"Didn't you think the schools were fascinating?"

"Did you think they were real?"

"Of course they were real."

"I mean, do you think it was a show, the way the students were so intent, the rooms so bright and sunny. The posters filled with polite English phrases on the walls, the way the teacher only had to nod his head and the students would sit or stand and answer, or whatever it was he wanted them to do?"

"Of course they knew we were coming…"

"To look at them, and judge them."

"We weren't there to judge, but to observe."

"How can you observe without judging?"

She tasted her sweetened tea, holding the hot glass by the edge of the rim with her thumb and middle finger, careful not to burn her fingers. She had come to like the very hot dark tea of Turkey and how refreshing it could be on a windless summer day.

"We all knew they were on their best behavior, they always are when people come to observe."

APRICOTS IN A TURKISH GARDEN

"No one likes to be judged."

"We weren't judging…"

"We're always watching, thinking, judging. Isn't that what makes us human? That and our opposable thumbs?"

Blowing across the surface of her tea in order to cool it slightly, Lisa took another sip. Her husband Jim looked out the window.

"As a journalist, I would have thought you would have jumped at the chance to write about that day in Taksim Square," she said, putting down her cup.

"Not exactly PC when you're there with your wife who has been asked to come as an educator/ambassador to the country to look at all their wonderful schools and their wonderful obedient children and their wonderful this and their wonderful that…"

"Is that what's stopping you?"

"Nothing is stopping me…"

"You said yourself that you didn't want to write about Turkey," she reminded him.

"We didn't see everything. They were too careful to show us only what they wanted us to see…"

"Didn't you find it interesting that the hotel clerk told us that morning before we left to see the city that we needed to be back at the hotel by 4 o'clock because the demonstration would be happening by then."

"And, as instructed, we came back and stood outside the doorway of our hotel watching people gather for the demonstration, like we were there to observe them just like we were there in their schools. Doesn't it bother you that they knew we were watching?"

"I hardly think anyone even knew who we were…"

"What *we* are you talking about?"

"The group of ambassadors we were with…that we. Which, by the way, included you."

"How about the big we? The outsiders, the news media, the Western Judeo-Christian we...the everyone who is not Muslim we, all of us watching, waiting for a riot, like we had front row seats to a hockey game and were just standing around hoping a fight would break out."

"And that's why you feel you can't write about Turkey, because you thought you would be judging them just like everyone else judges them if you wrote about it?"

"I don't really know what we saw that day anymore than I know what we saw when we visited those schools. Do you?"

"Do I what?"

"Know what you saw?"

"I saw the same thing you saw."

"Did you?"

"We were there, together..."

"Did you see the angry shouting mob CNN reported in the news the next day?"

Lisa ran her fingers down the warm curved sides of her glass, gathering her thoughts and thinking. The waiter saw her looking at her glass and held up his teapot in question. Lisa shook her head, no.

"I saw the men and women get out of the tunnel and walk quietly together down the wide shopping street to the Park. I did not hear them shouting,"

"Neither did I," Jim said.

"I was surprised there were so many."

"Istanbul is a big city."

"It was four o'clock in the afternoon on a Tuesday."

"Do you think they were angry?"

"Determined, maybe, but not angry."

"Happy and determined like all those students we saw?"

"You're confusing the two things, they're not the same."

"Are you sure?"

Lisa wasn't sure anymore if they were having a conversation or a fight.

"What's your point?" she asked, motioning for the waiter to freshen her tea.

The waiter came to the table and once again performed the ritual tall pouring of the tea. The two of them sat silently as they watched. There was a sense of magic to it, even though they had seen him and all the waiters in Turkey do it time and time again. Lisa took two more large lumps of sugar and stirred them into her glass.

"My point is that I'm not sure anymore what I saw either in the classrooms or on the streets of Istanbul, and it bothers me."

"It's such a beautiful country," she offered, once again picking up her tea glass so as not to burn her fingers.

"Beautiful and fragile."

"I didn't see that," she said.

"It haunts me," he said.

"What a strange thing to say," she said.

"Don't you think about it?"

"Of course," she said, offended that he might think her shallow.

"Both the students and the demonstrators were trying so hard to either show us something or hide something, I'm not even sure which one anymore."

"Maybe if you wrote about it…"

"What do you think I should say?"

"I don't care, just something about what we saw, what we did…"

"So, you agree, they asked me to come so I would write about it," Jim said.

"I just think that if something is bothering you, haunting you, like you just said, that you should do something about it so you can get on with things…"

"We should get our check," Jim said, lifting his hand to get the waiter's attention, signaling for the check.

"Was there anything?" she asked.

"I want to write about?"

"That you felt sure of?"

Jim took the check, glanced at it, pulled two tens and a five from his wallet and handed them to the waiter, waving his hand in order to indicate he didn't want the change.

The waiter made a slight bow and turned away from the table.

"Anything I felt sure of?" he asked.

"Yes," she answered.

"There was one thing," he said.

"What?"

"That day in the garden," he said.

"Where the family had made us lunch, and the father, after we had eaten, took us outside to see his garden," she said.

"There was a row of apricot trees along the edge of the garden and the branches of the trees were burdened down with hundreds of tiny golden apricots the size of shooter marbles. There was a piece of cardboard near the trees where someone had split several dozen of the tiny apricots in half and pitted them, opening them up so the tender flesh was exposed," he went on.

"The man said he was drying them and he told you to try one…"

"It was late in the afternoon, and the air was just beginning to stir with the slightest breeze and I could smell the roses in the garden and the breath of the coming cool night air. I remembered thinking that I had never felt so sure of having my feet firmly planted on the earth before, yet so far away from the rest of the world, and when I put the apricot in my mouth it was still alive and warm from the sun."